The true gestation period of a photograph is not the seconds, or fraction of seconds, of exposure, but rather the years the photographer has spent on a journey that is both physical and intellectual before reaching the point when the shutter was opened."

-- David Ward

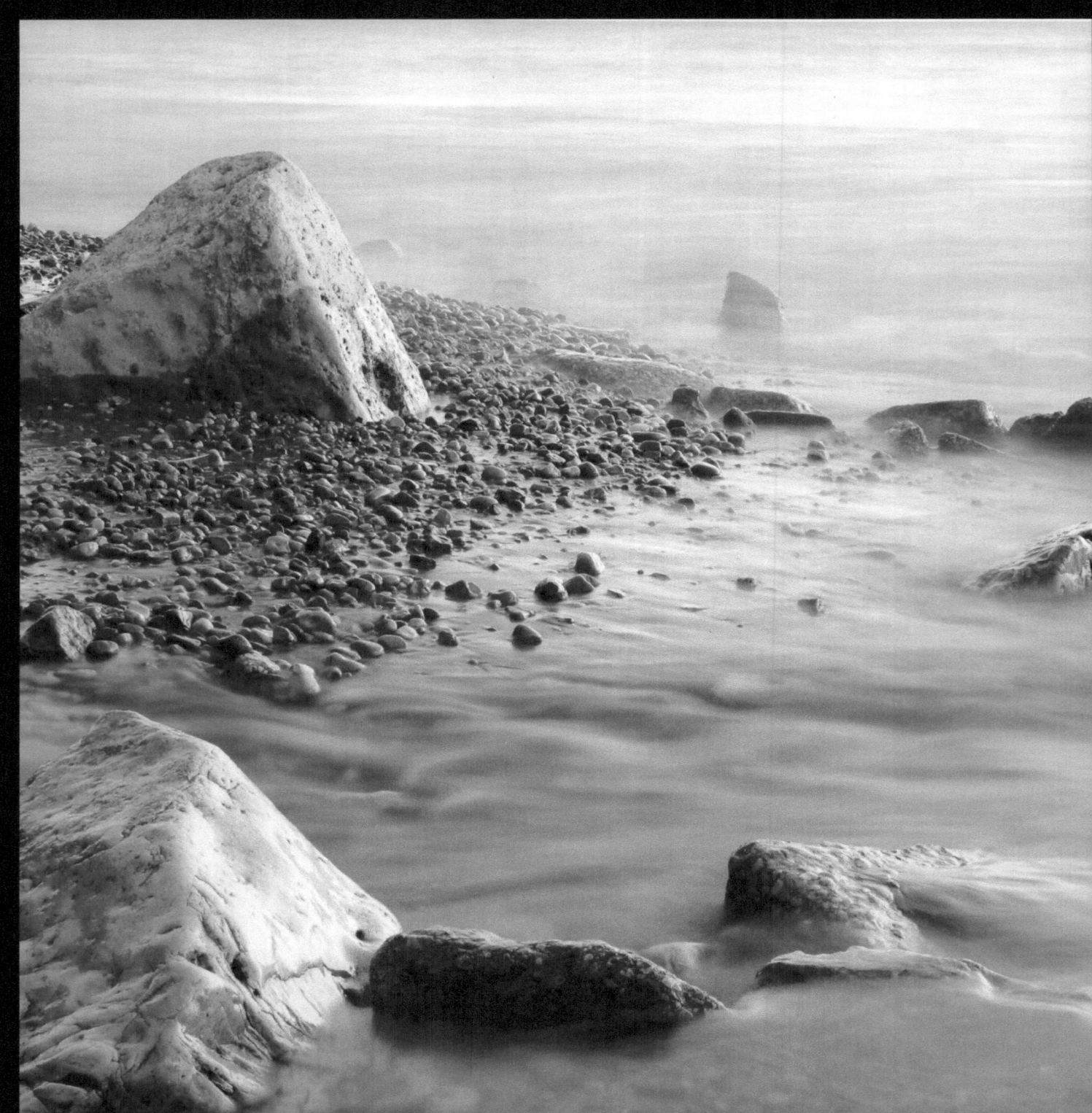

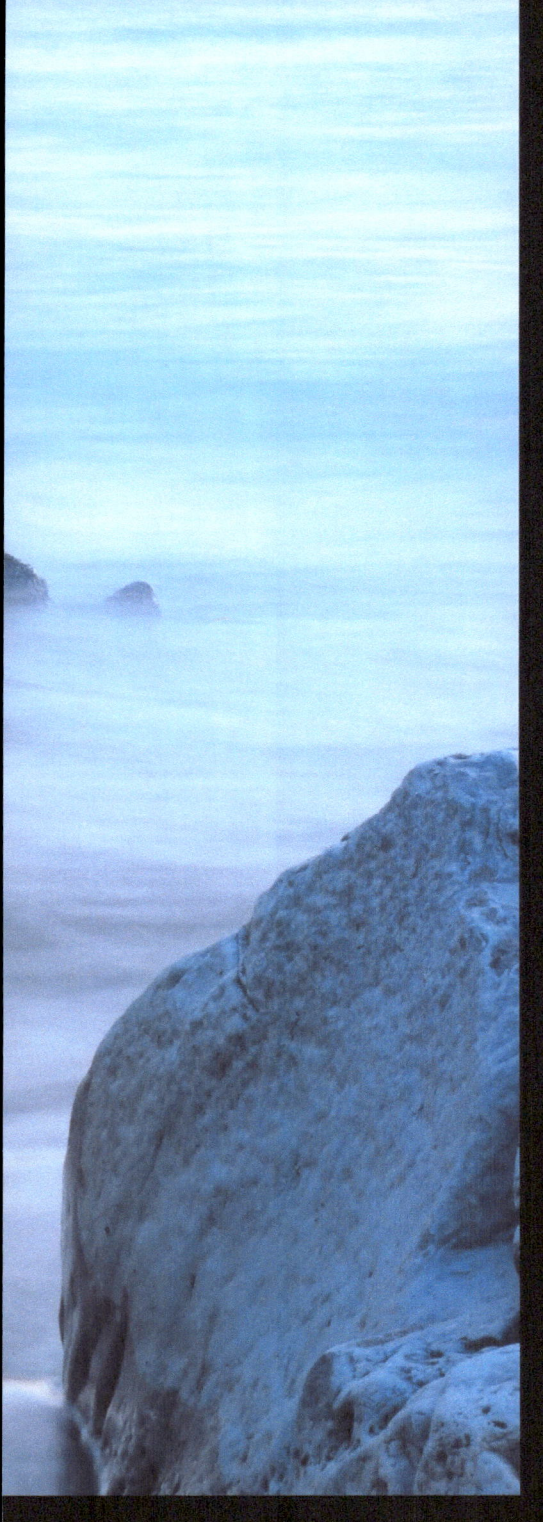

"Live, travel, adventure, bless and don't be sorry."

-- Jack Kerouac

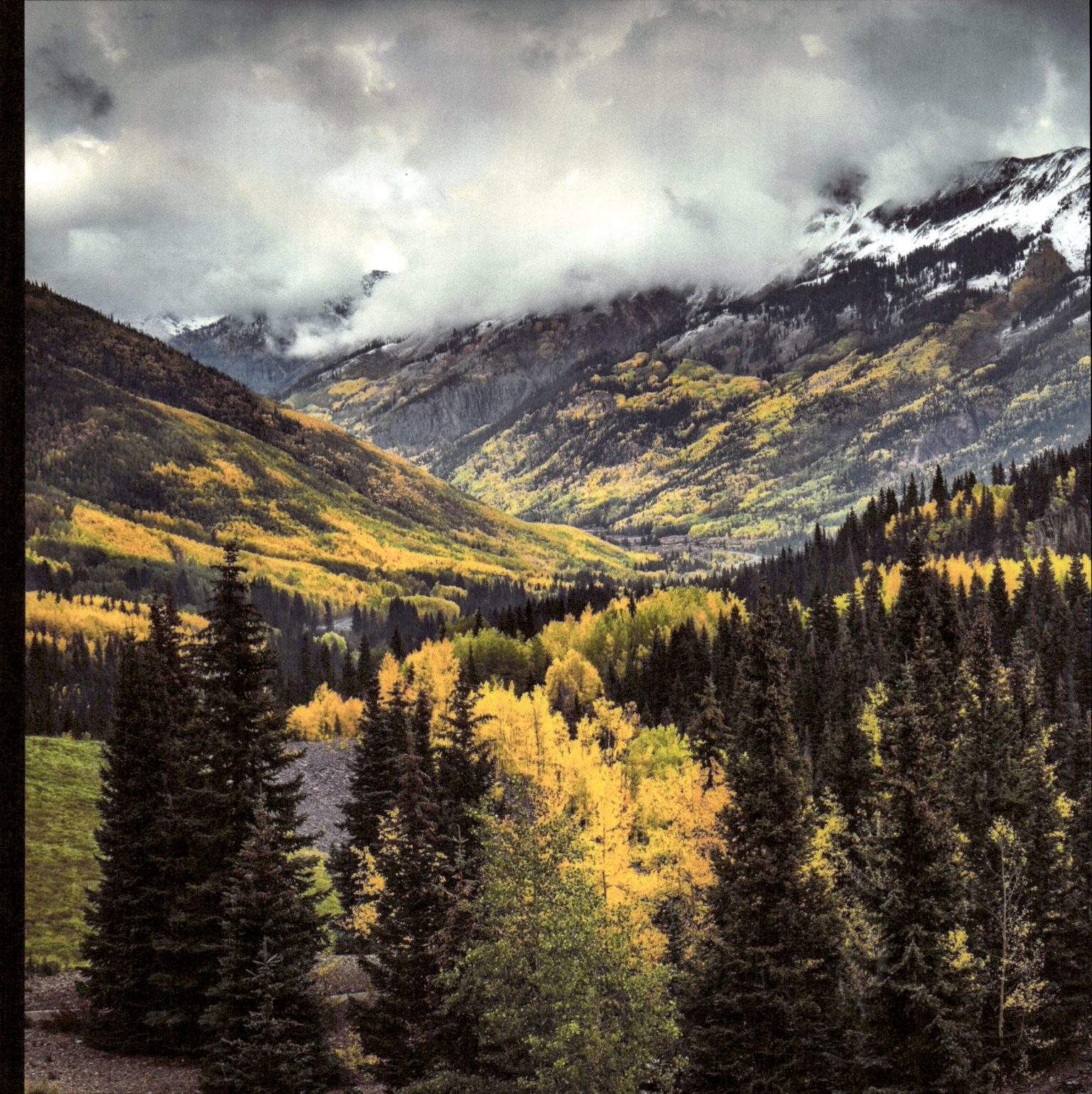

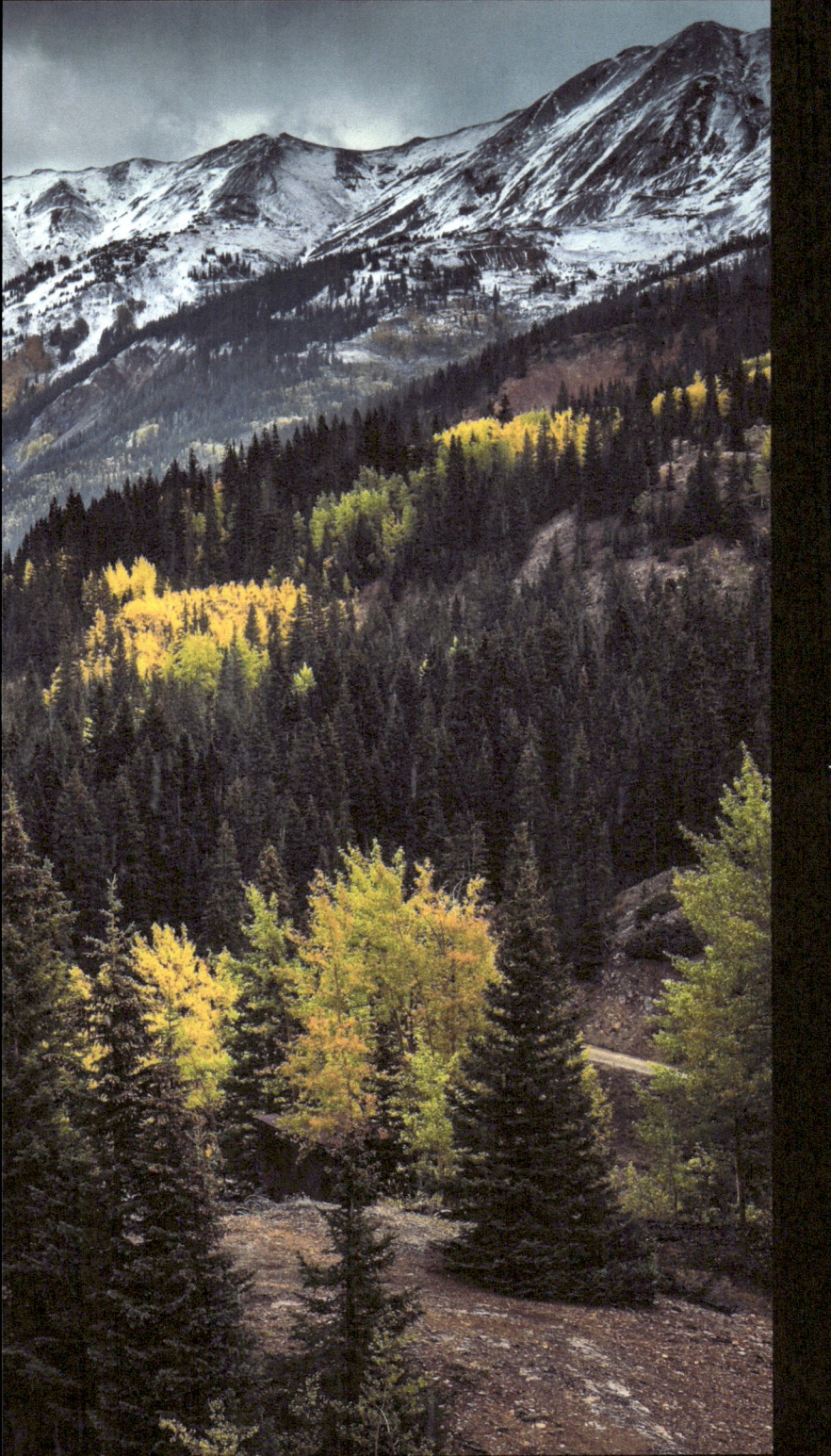

There are no short cuts to the places worth going to.

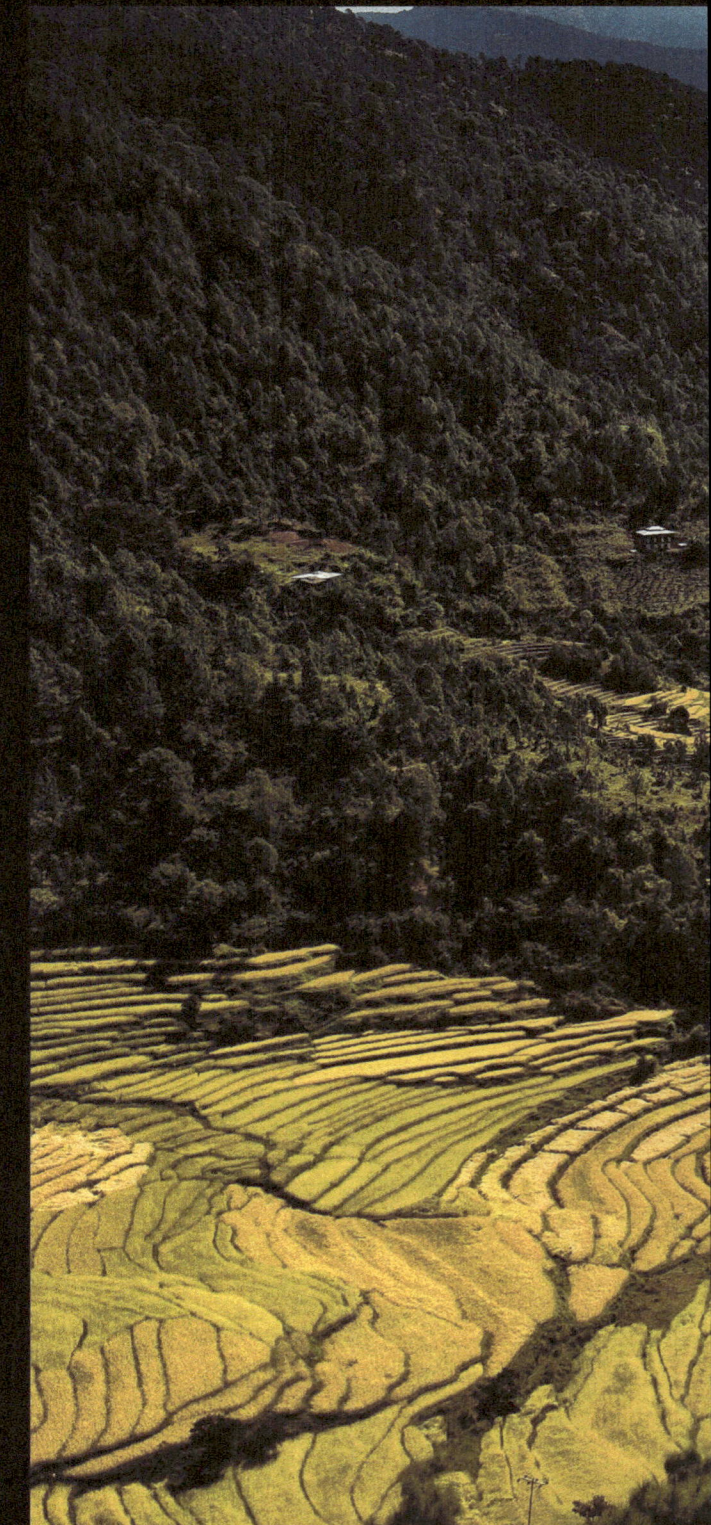

"And the end of all our exploring will be to arrive where we started, and know the place for the first time.

-- T. S. Elliot

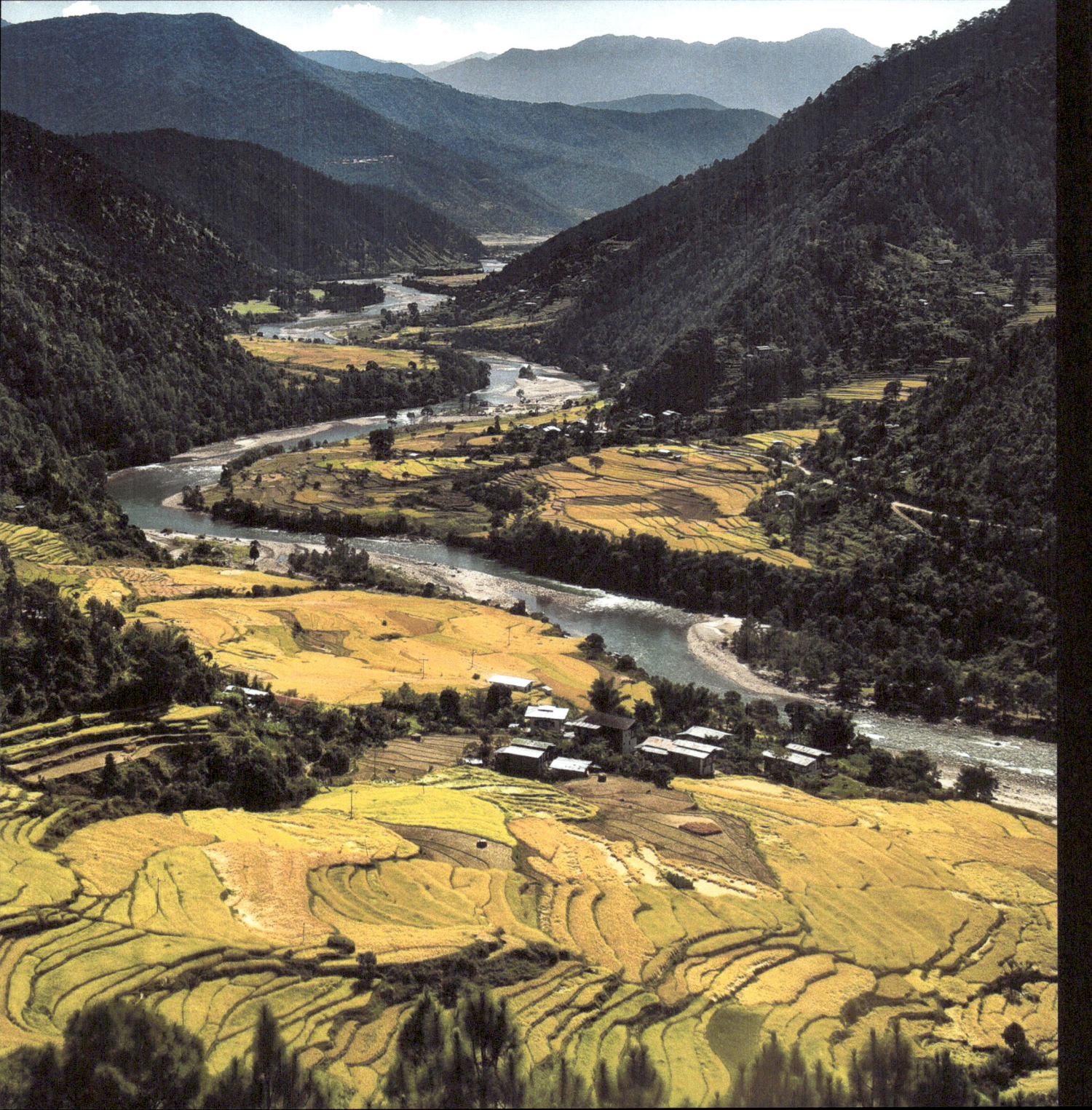

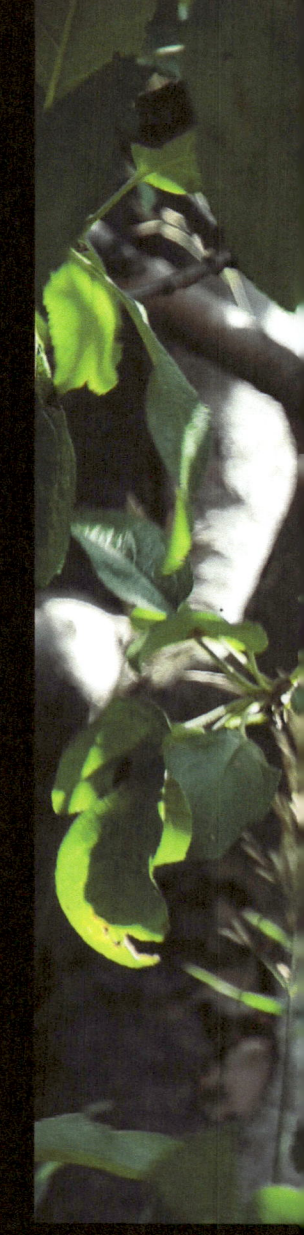

"There are only two
ways to live your life.
One is as though
nothing is a miracle.
The other is as though
everything is a miracle."

-- Albert Einstein

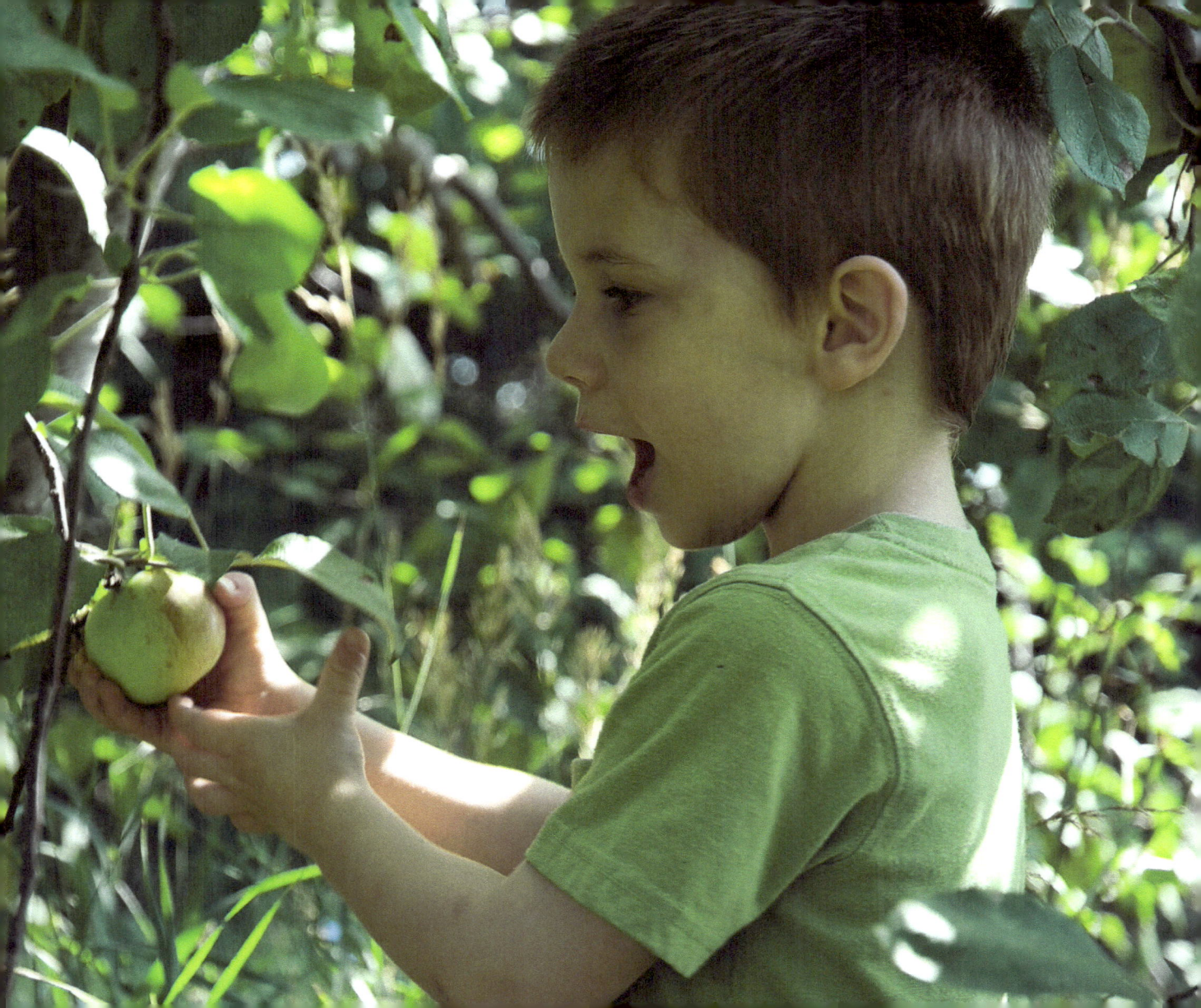

"Wind extinguishes a candle
and energizes a fire."

-- Nassim Taleb

"When I was a child, my mother used to say to me over and over again, 'Pablo, if you become a soldier you will be a general and if you become a priest you will be Pope.' But I became an artist, and so, I became Picasso."

--Pablo Picasso

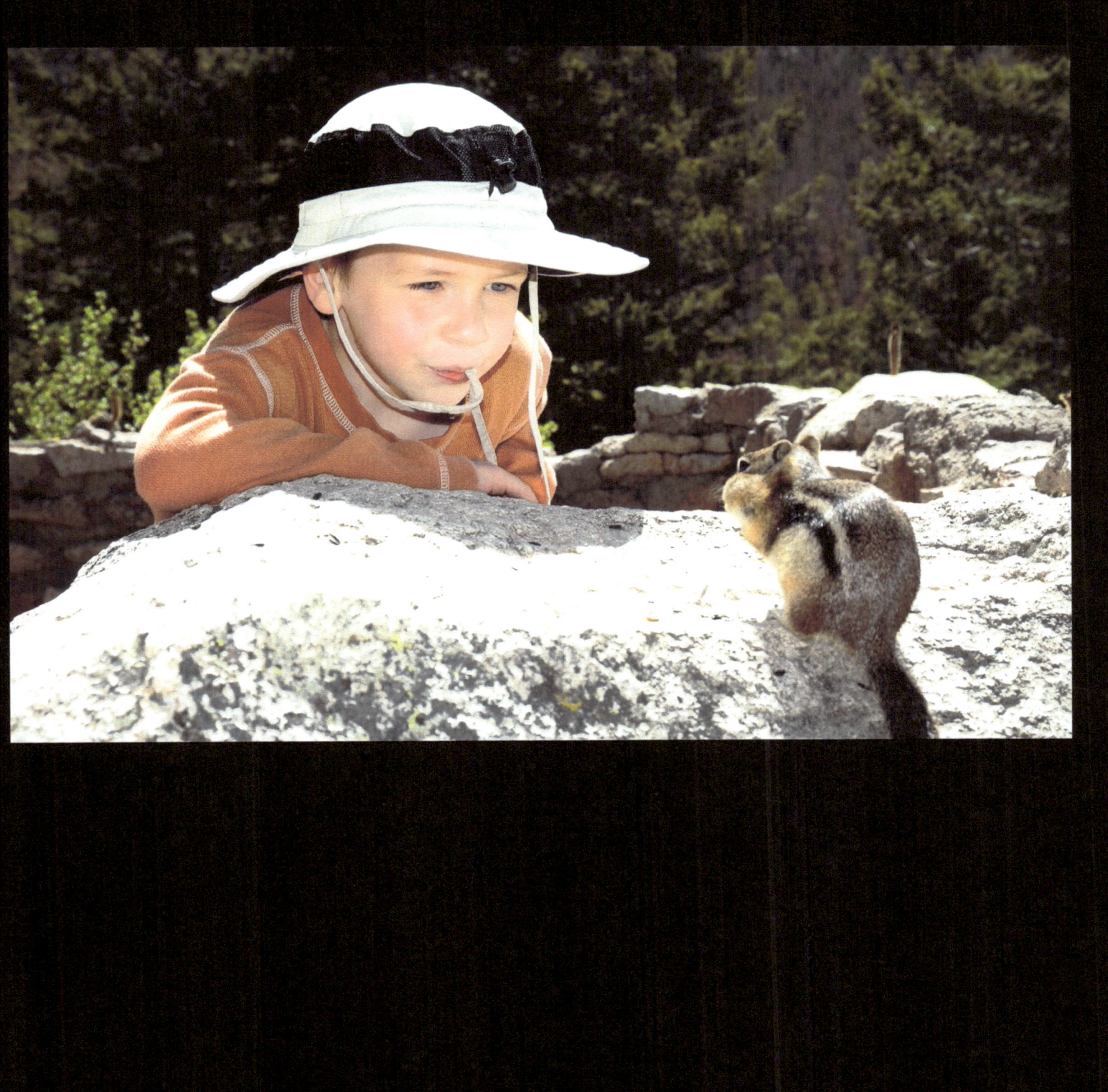

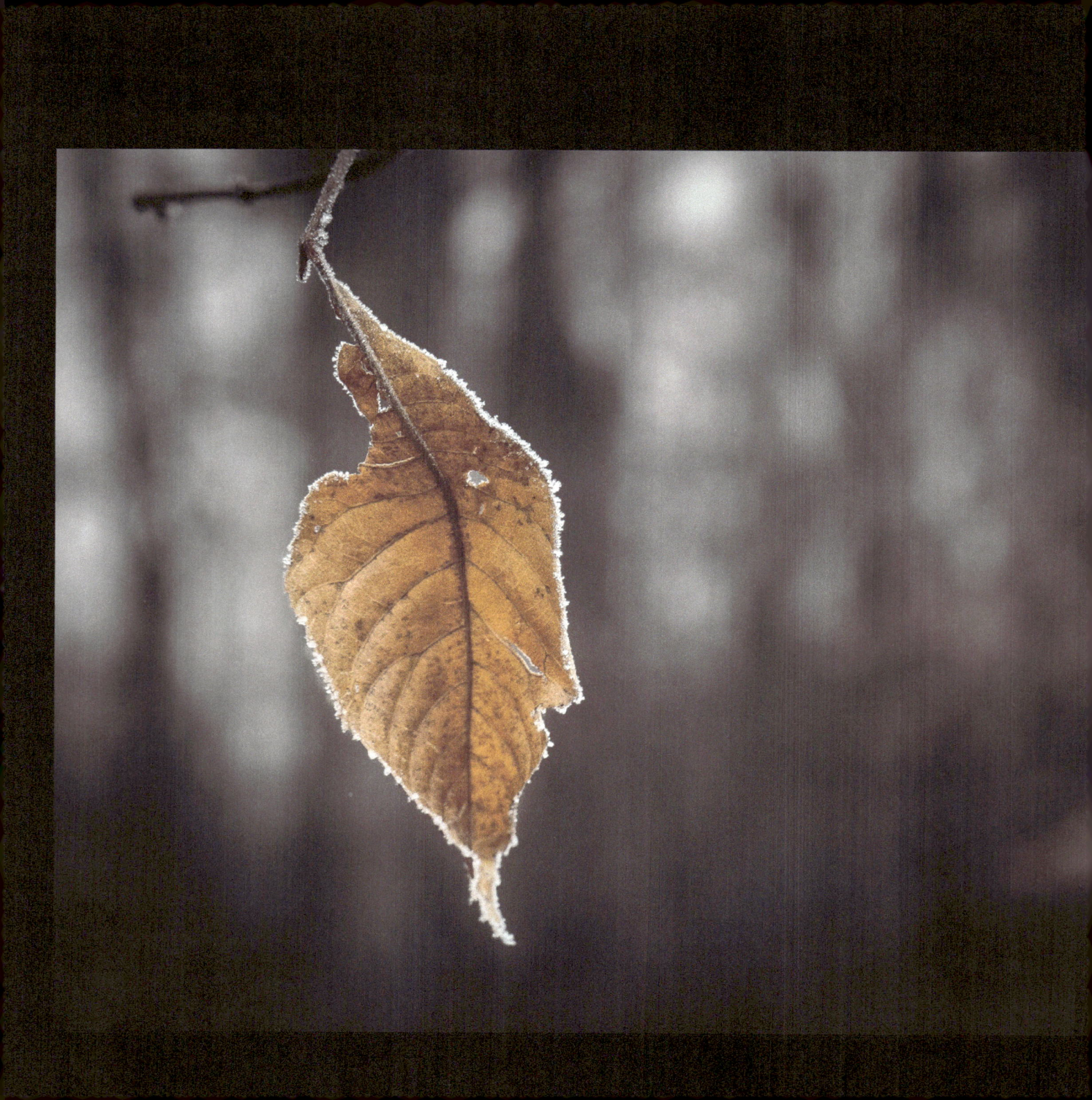

"Beware the barrenness of a busy life."

-- Socrates

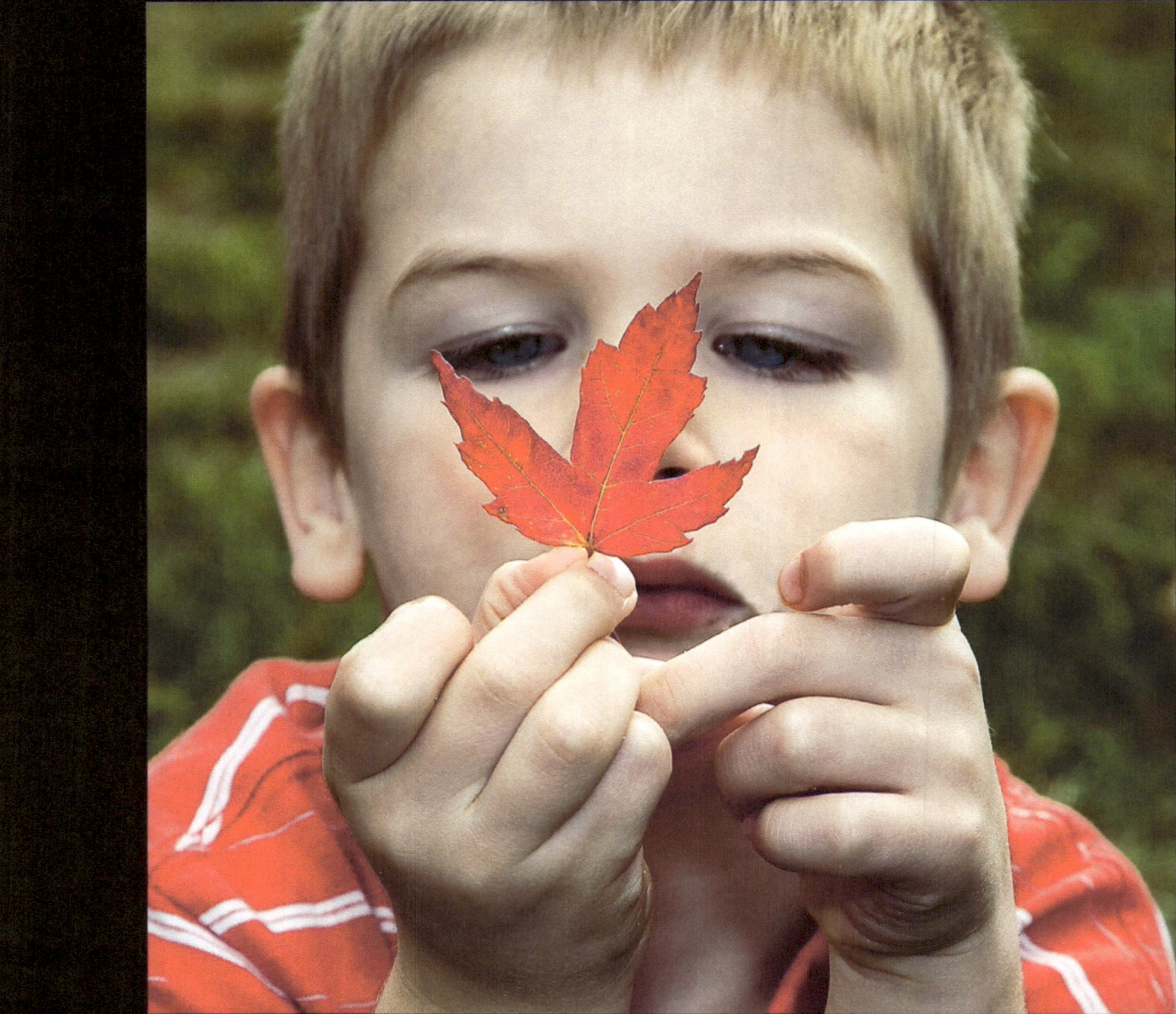

"The struggle of maturity is
to recover the seriousness
of a child at play."

-- Friedrich Nietzsche

"Every child is an artist, the
problem is how to remain
an artist once we grow up."

--Pablo Picasso

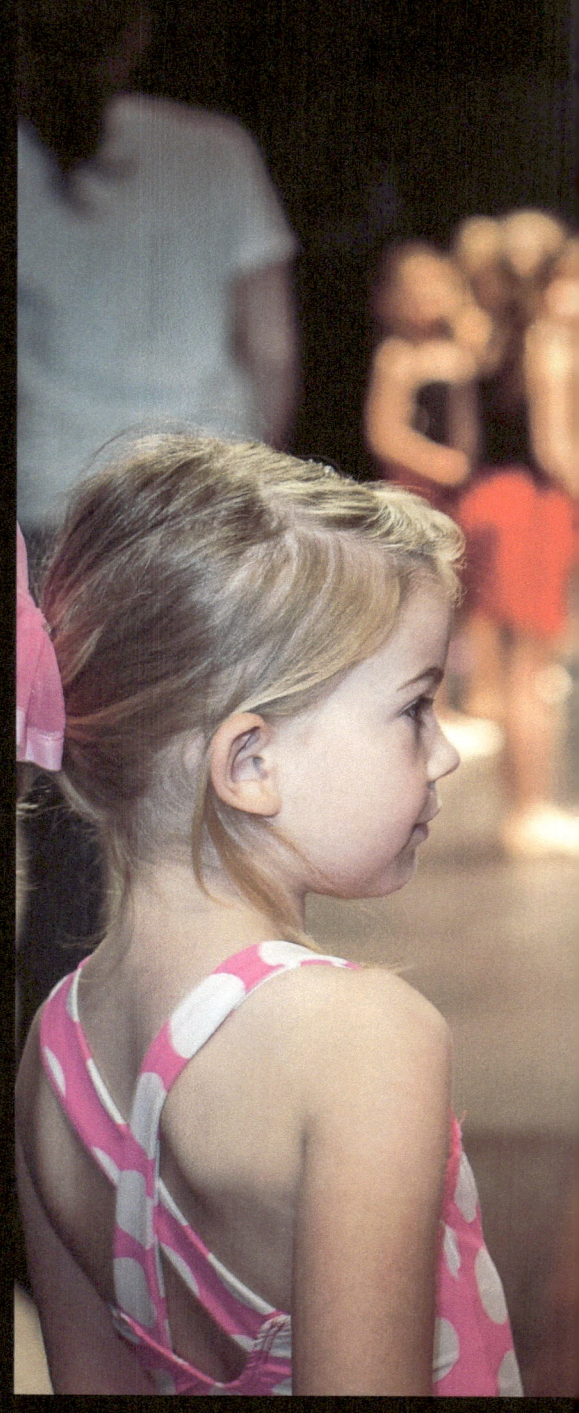

"[Life] is a dance, and when you are dancing, you are not intent on getting somewhere. The meaning and purpose of dancing is the dance.

-- Alan Watts

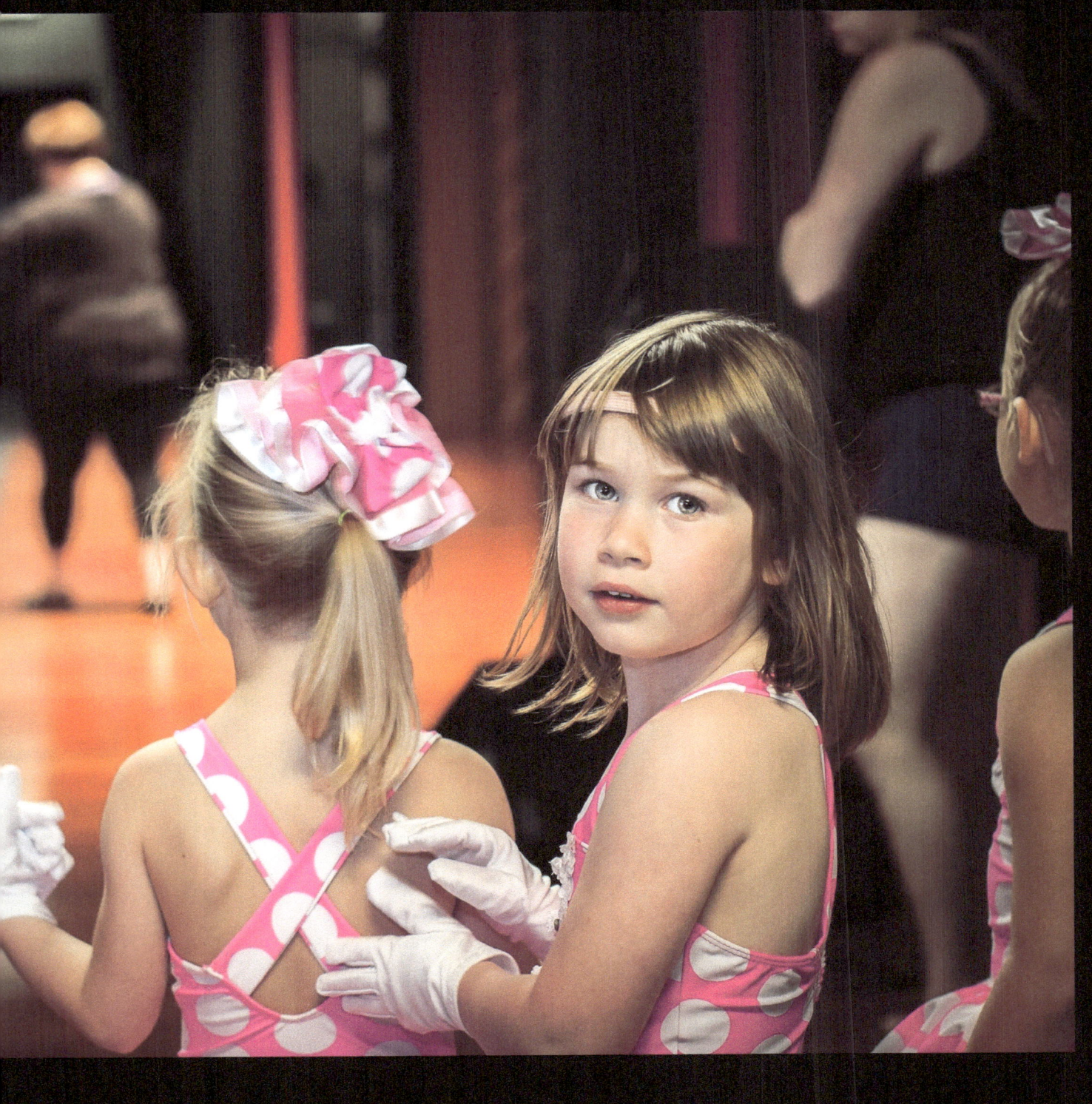

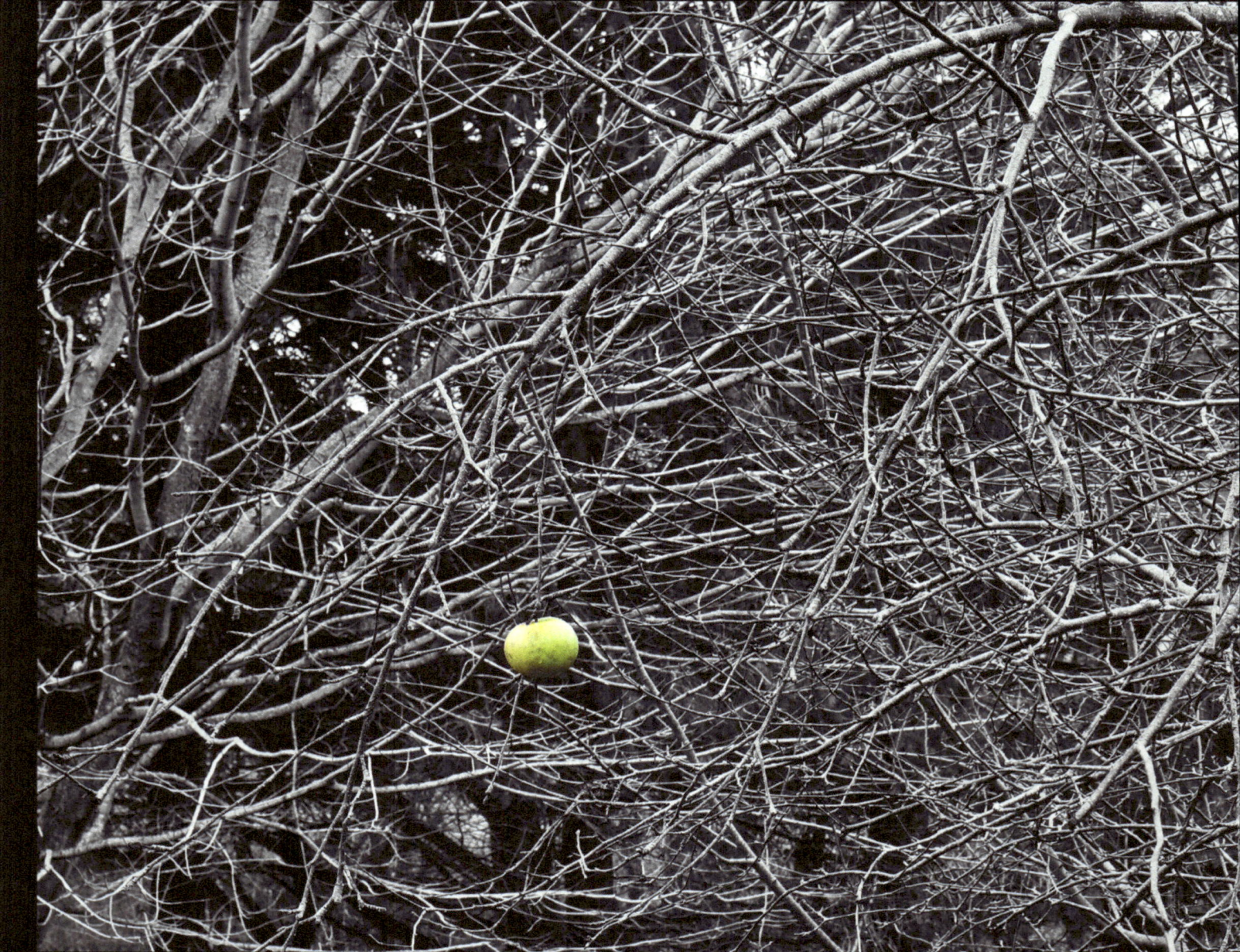

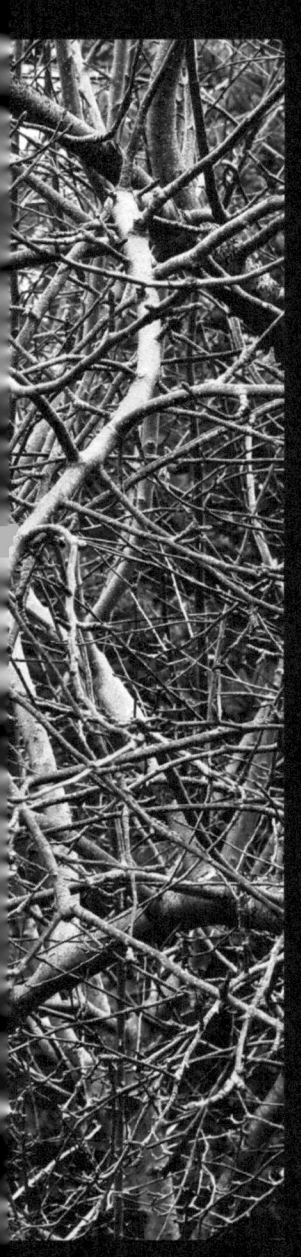

"One day you will wake up and there won't be any more time to do the things you've always wanted to do. *Do them now!*"

-- Paulo Coelho

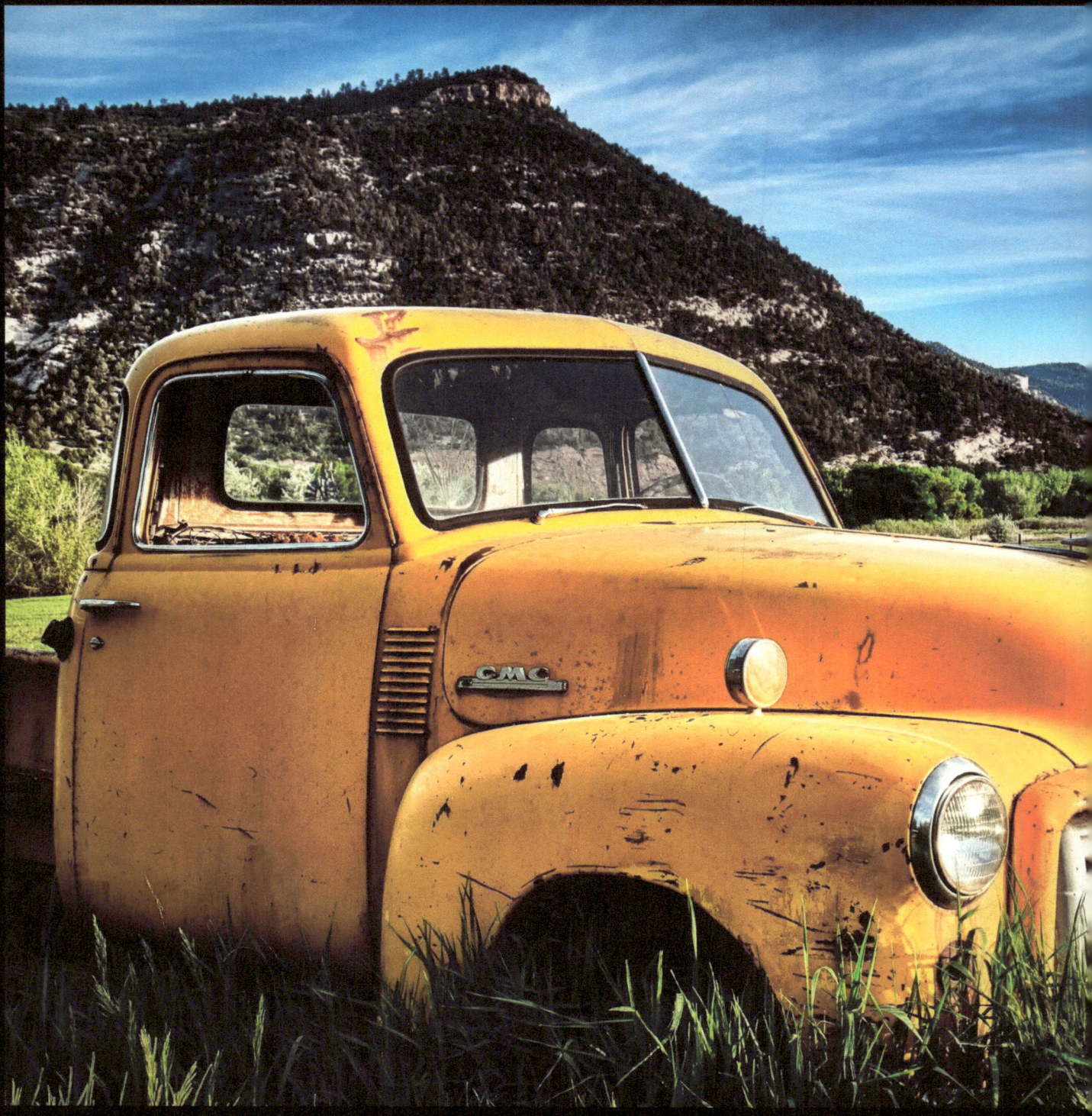

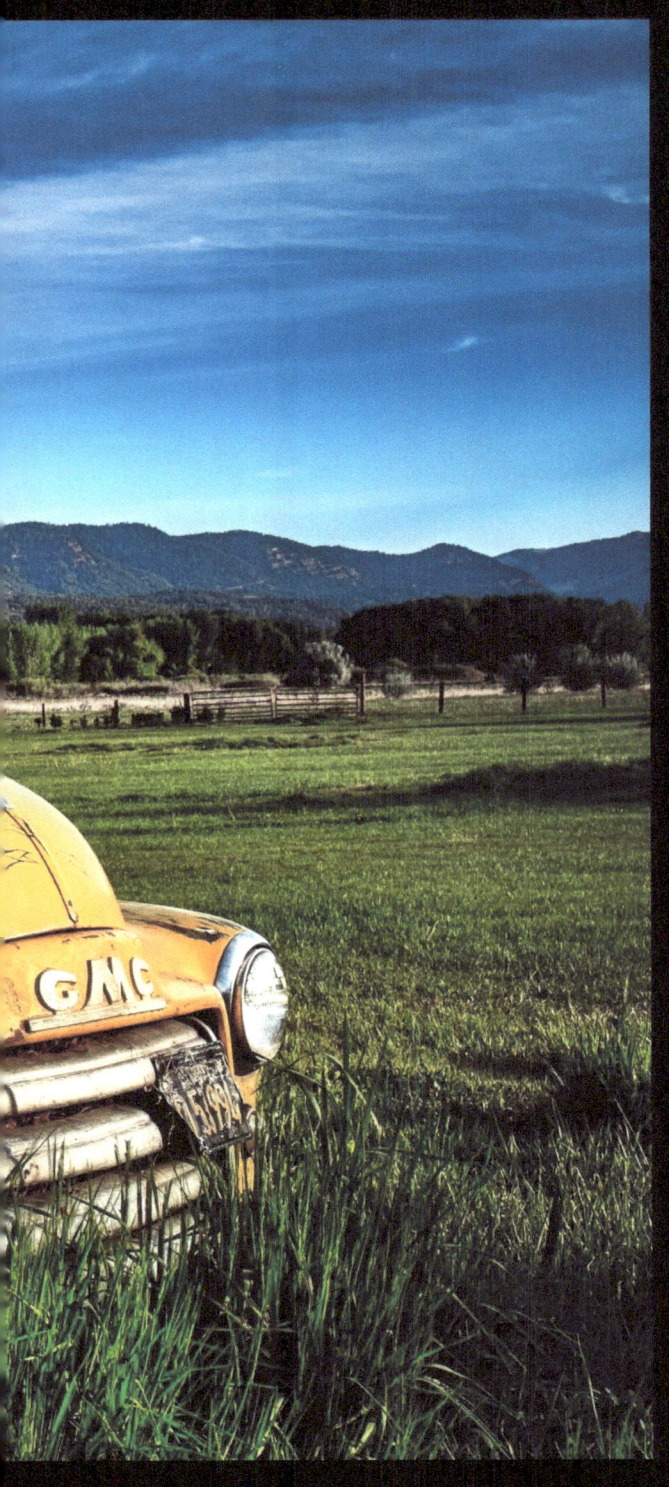

"The danger for most of us is not that our aim is too high and we miss it, but that it is too low and we reach it."

--Michelangelo

"Not all who wander are lost."

--J.R.R. Tolkien

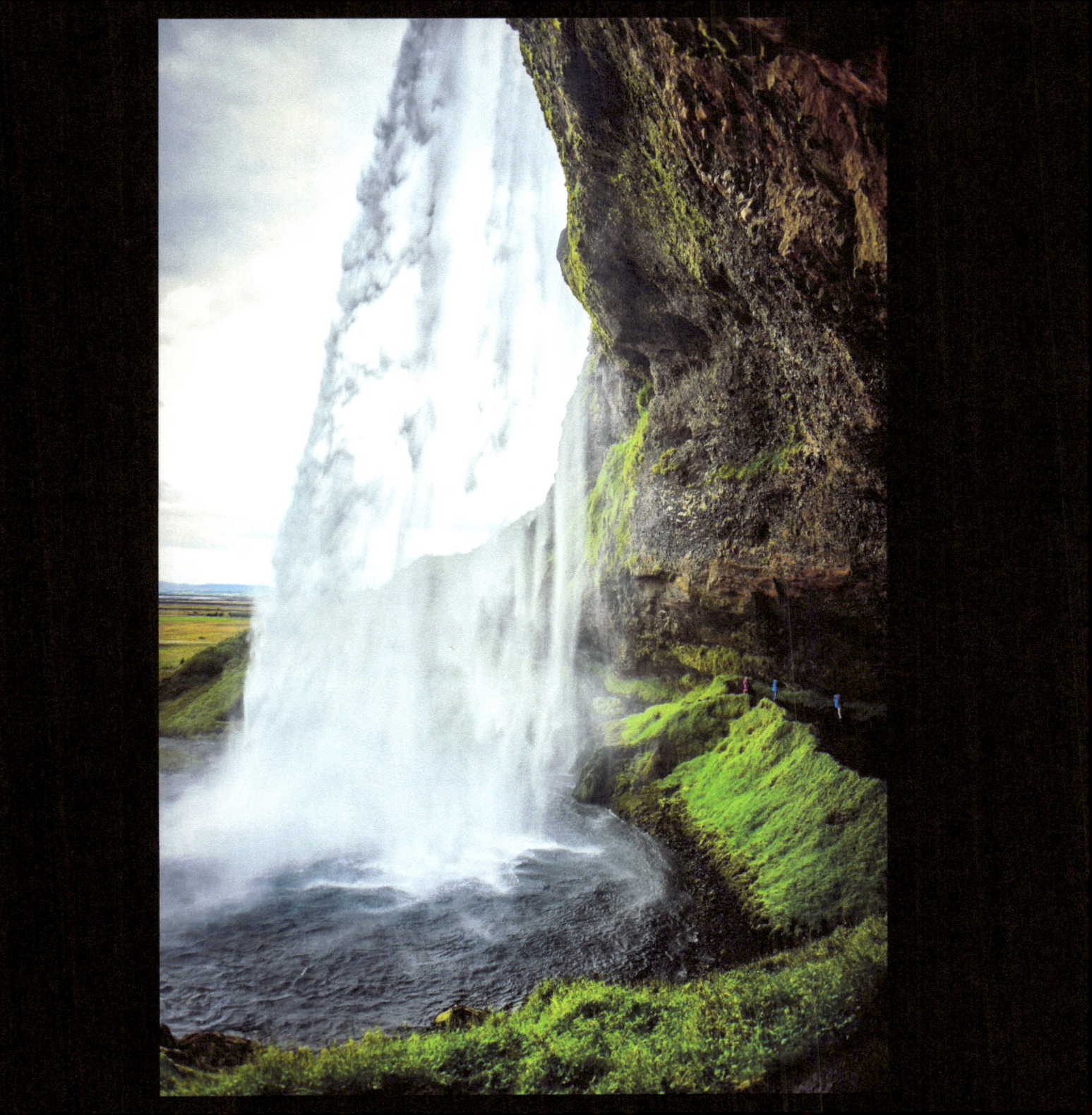

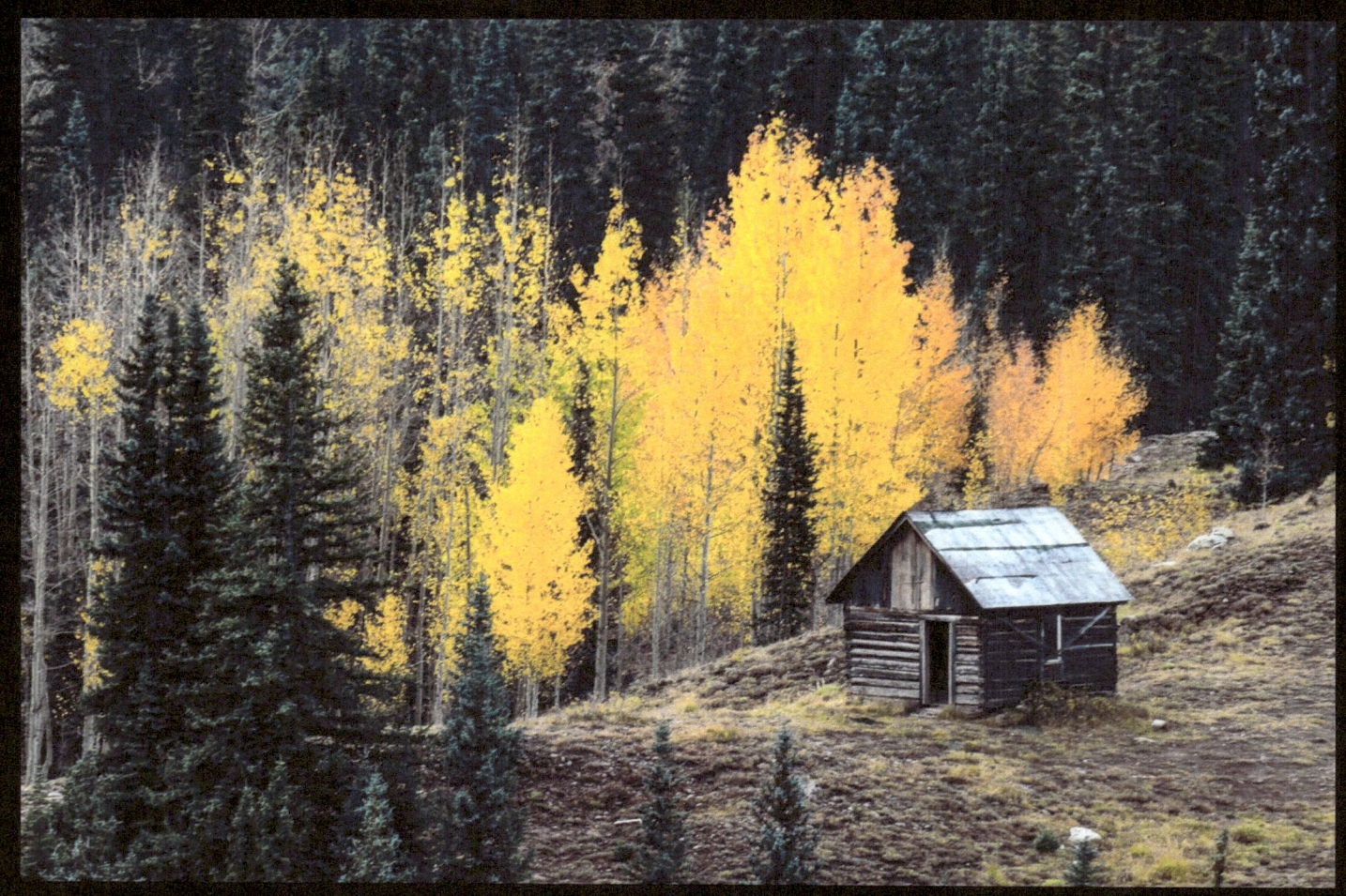

"Travel is fatal to prejudice, bigotry and narrow-mindedness."

-- Mark Twain

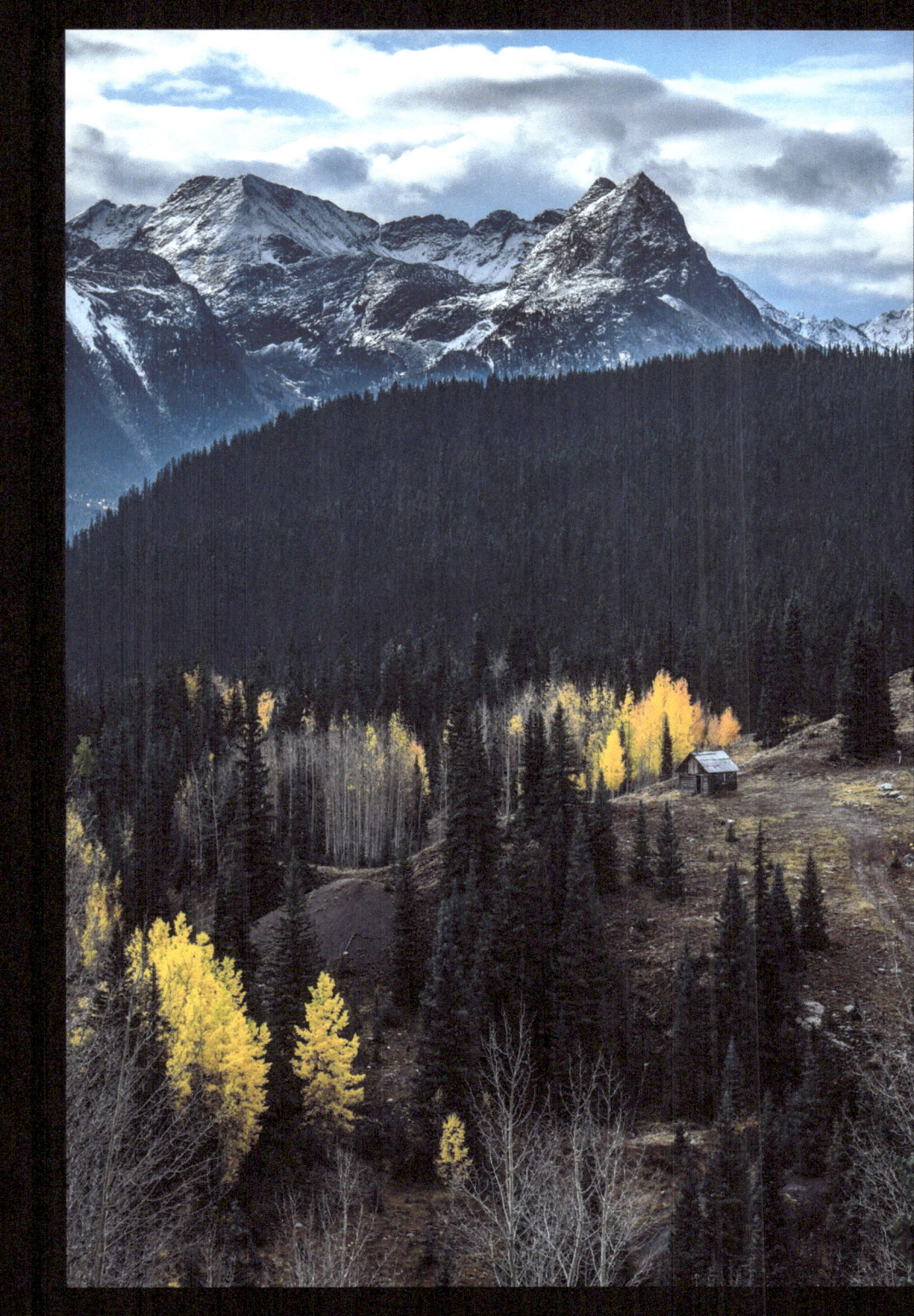

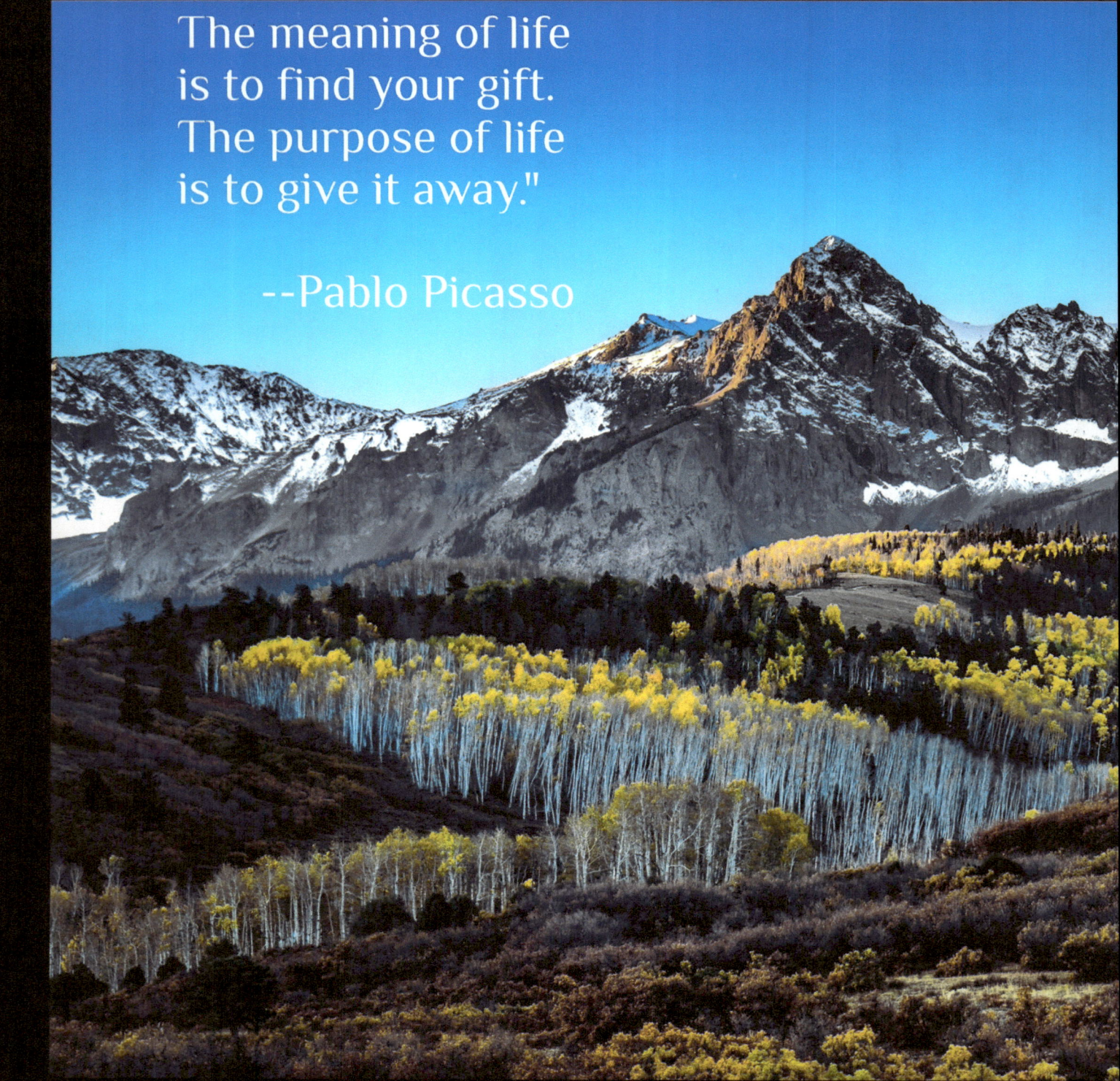

The meaning of life
is to find your gift.
The purpose of life
is to give it away."

--Pablo Picasso

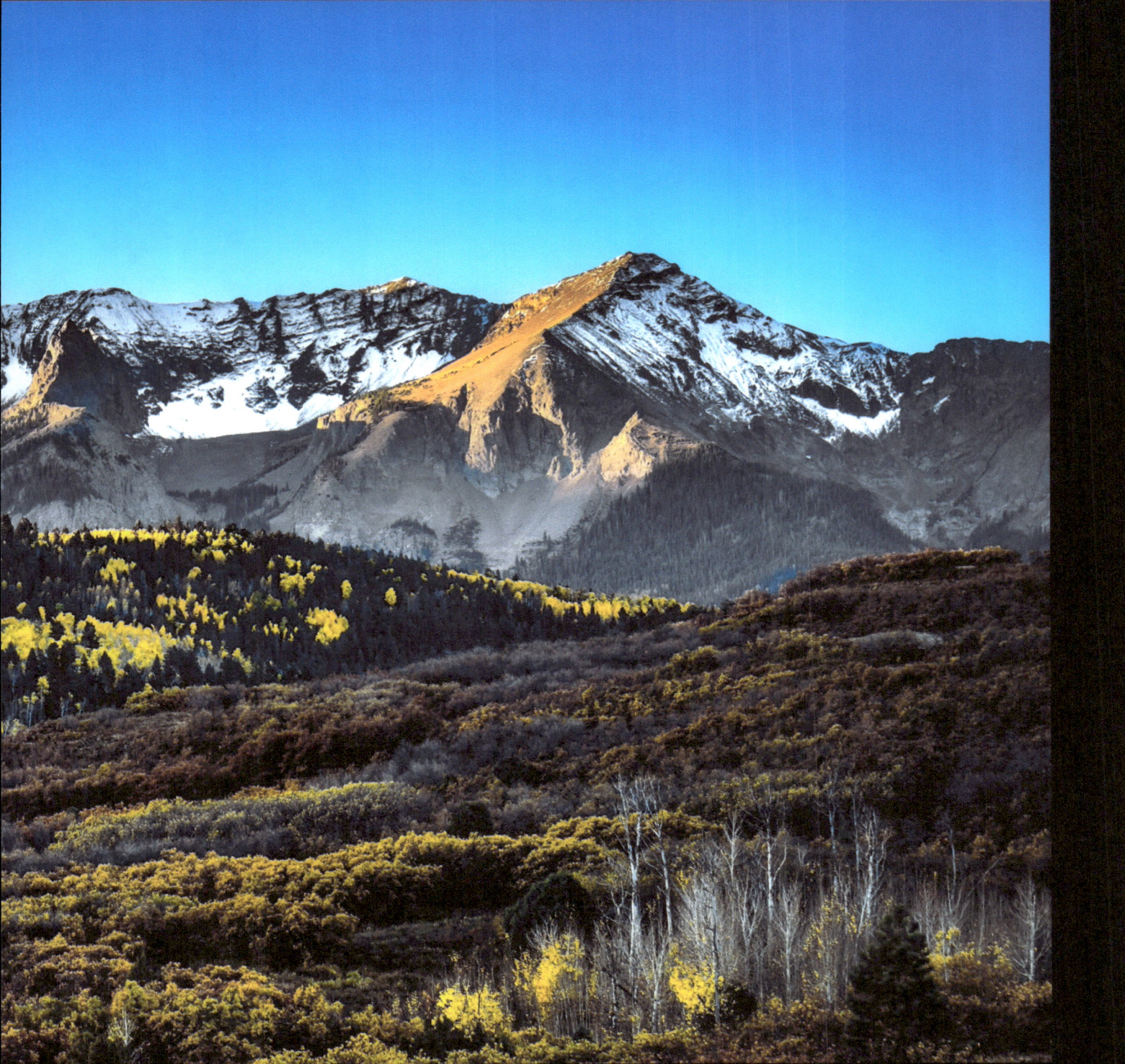

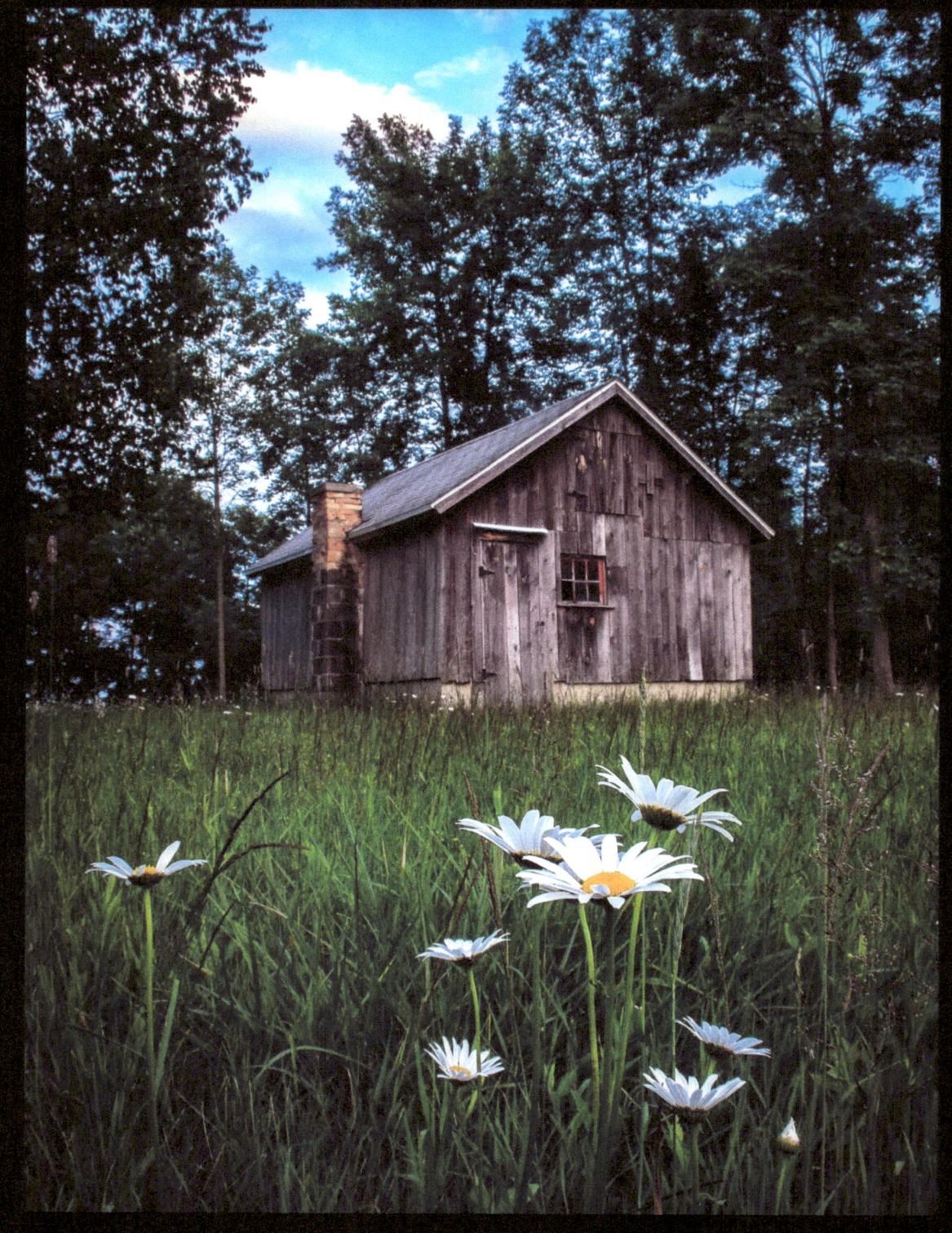

"If you love a flower, don't pick it up. Because if you pick it up it dies and ceases to be what you love.

So if you love a flower, let it be.

Love is not about possession.

Love is about appreciation."

--Osho

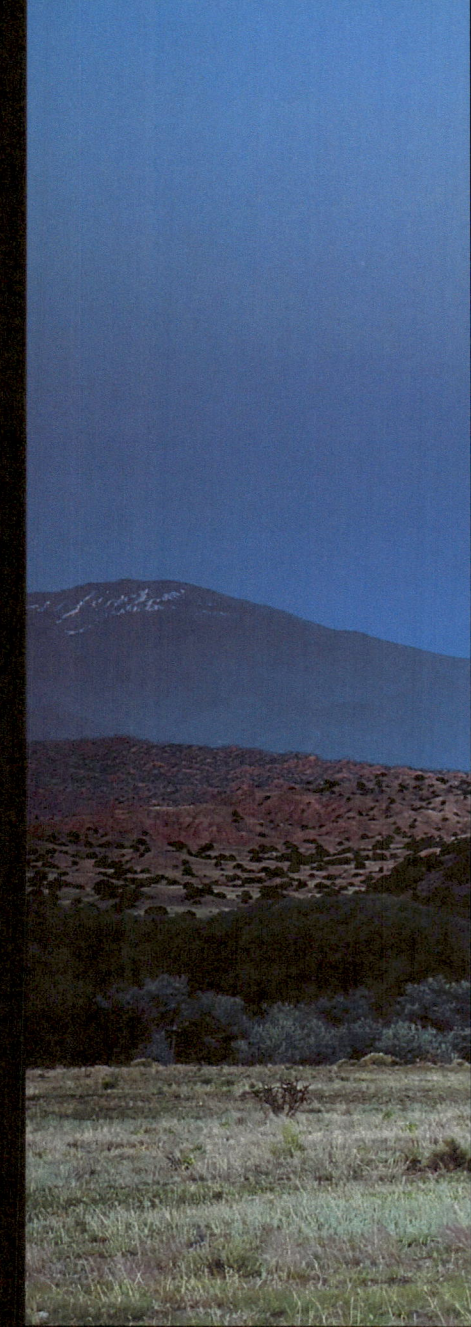

"People say that what we're seeking is a meaning for life. I don't think that's what we're really seeking. What we're seeking is an experience of being alive."

--Joseph Campbell

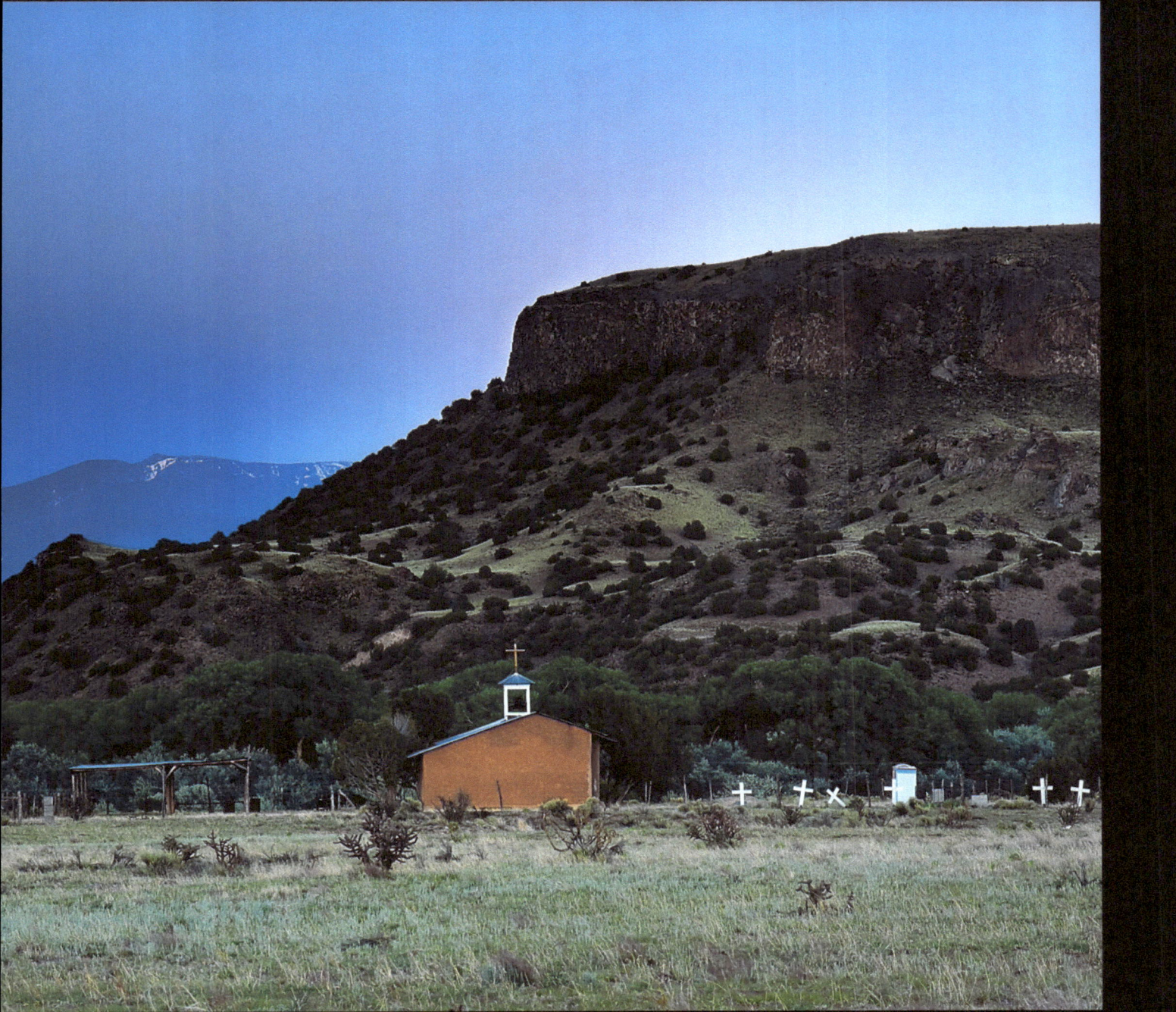

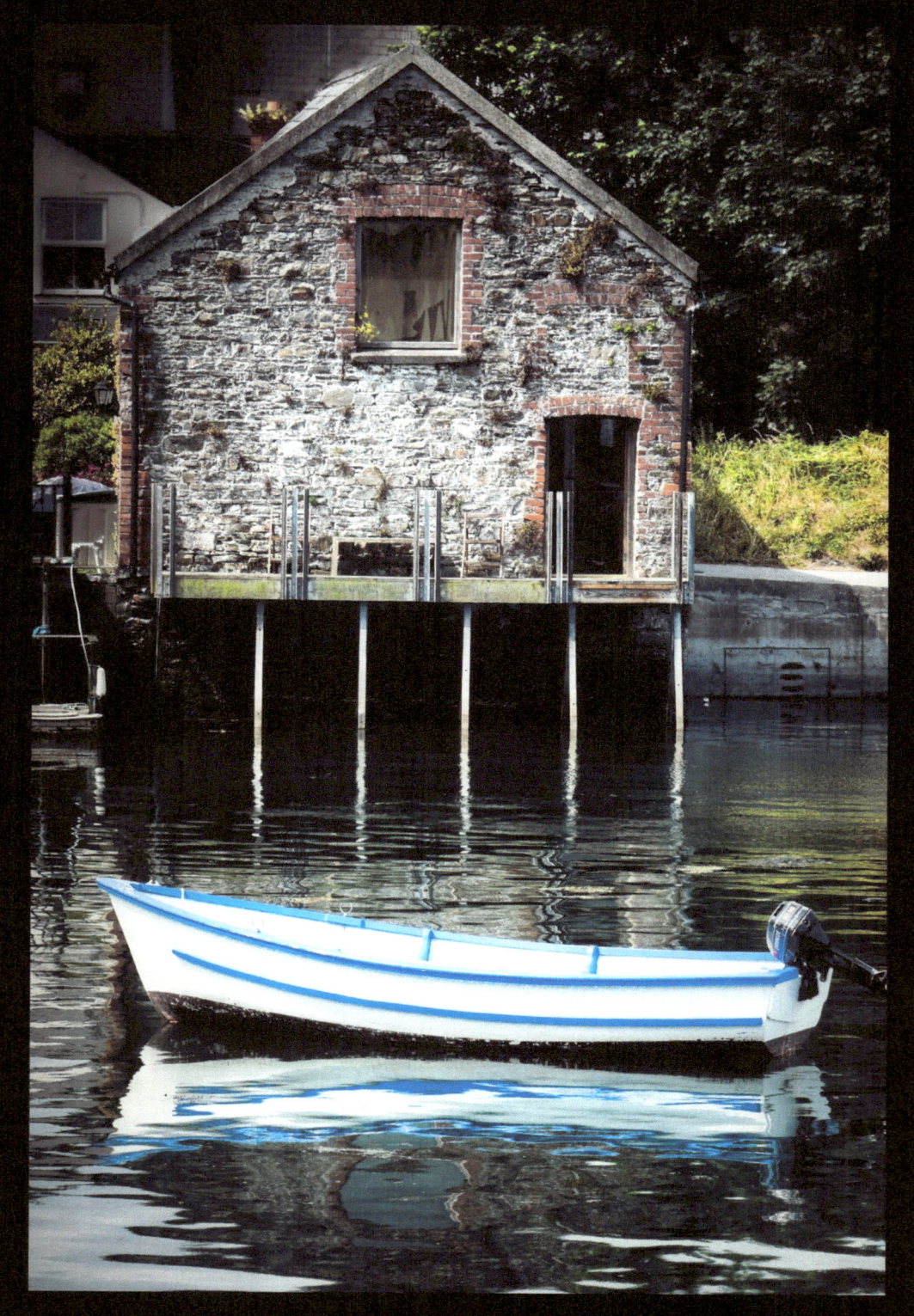

Twenty years from now you will be more disappointed by the things that you didn't do than by the ones you did do. So throw off the bowlines. Sail away from the safe harbor. Catch the trade winds in your sails.
Explore.
Dream.
Discover.

-- Mark Twain

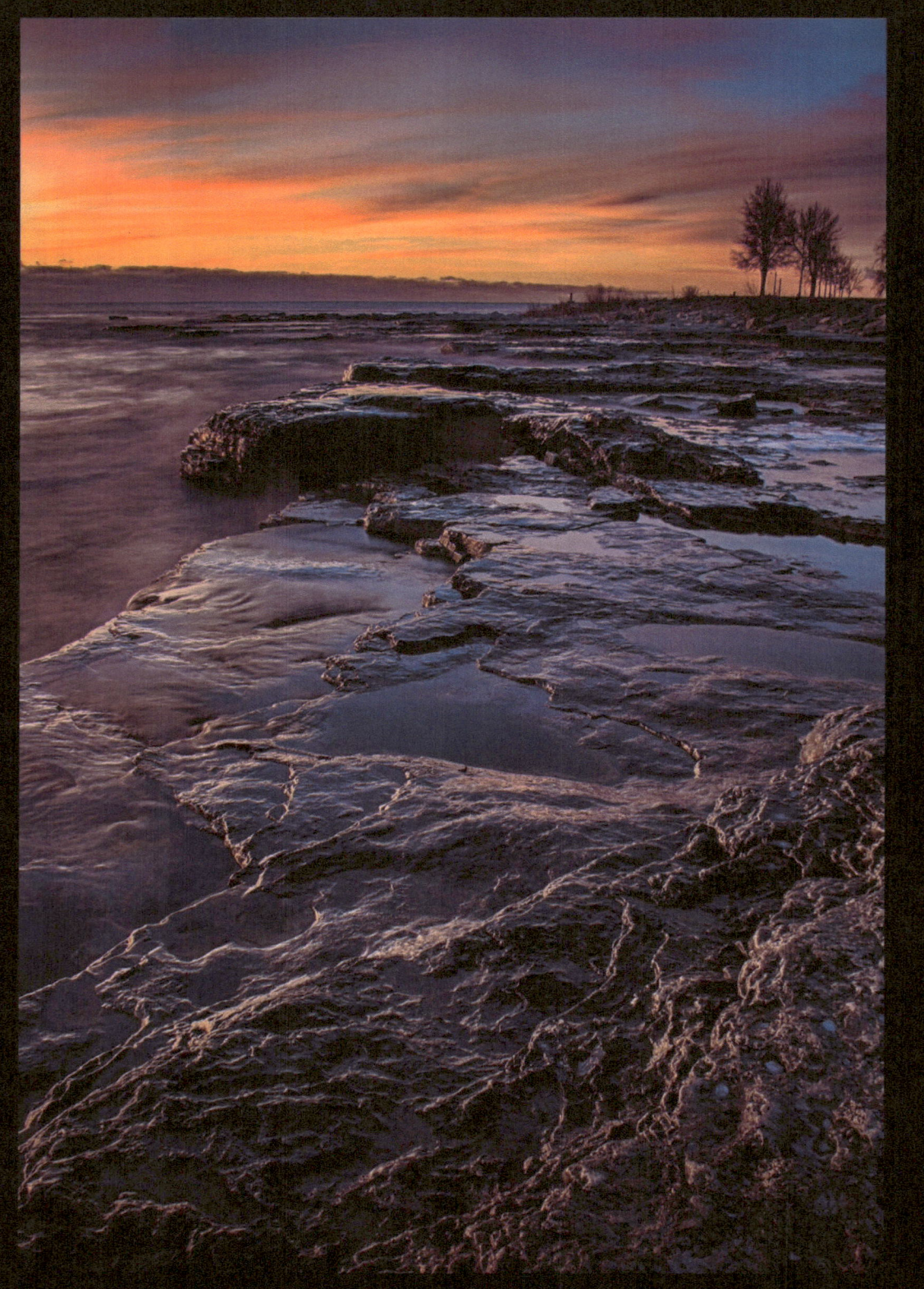

"One does not discover new lands without consenting to lose sight of the shore for a very long time."

--Andre Gide

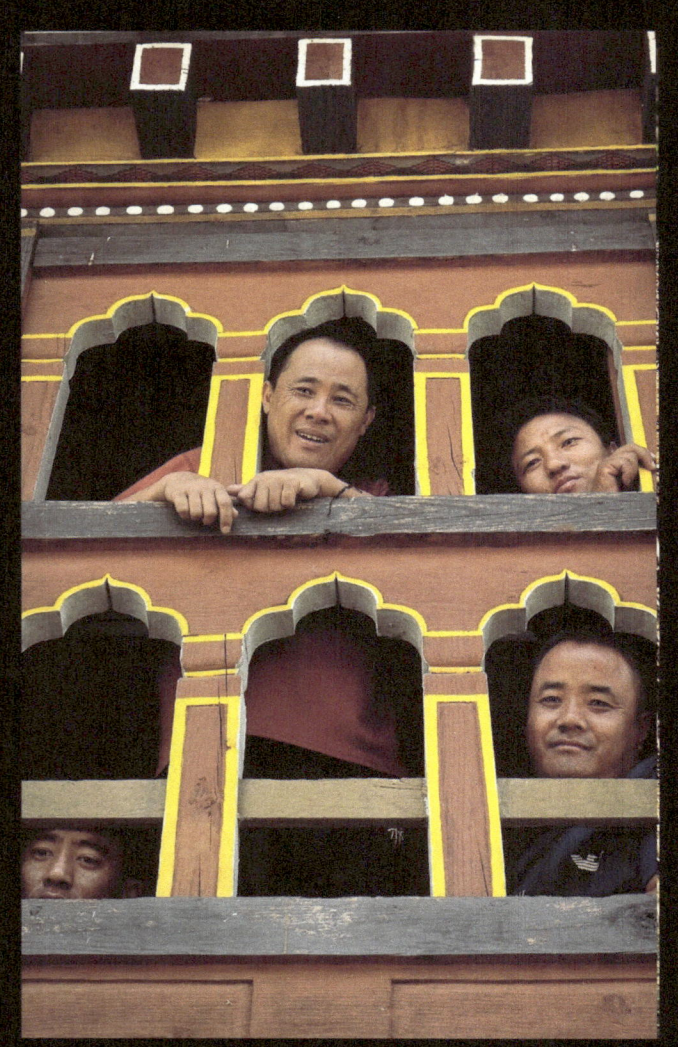

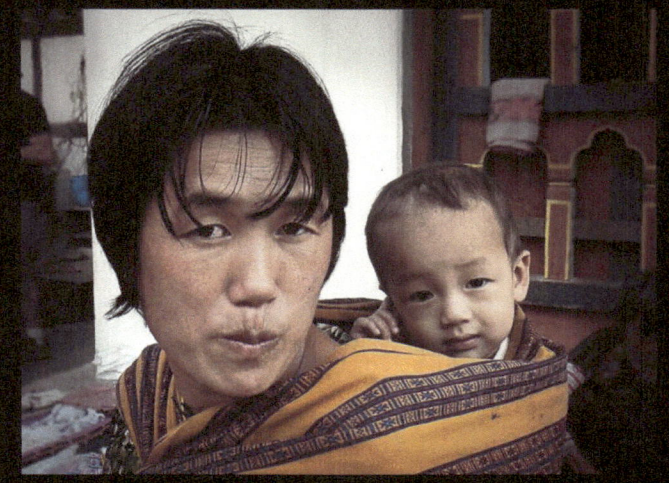

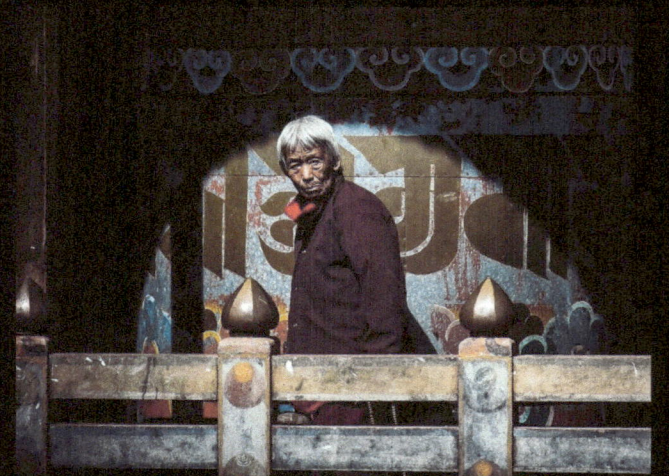

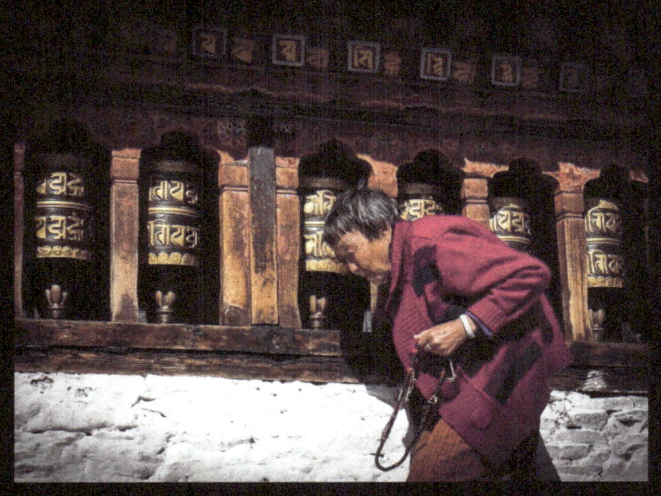

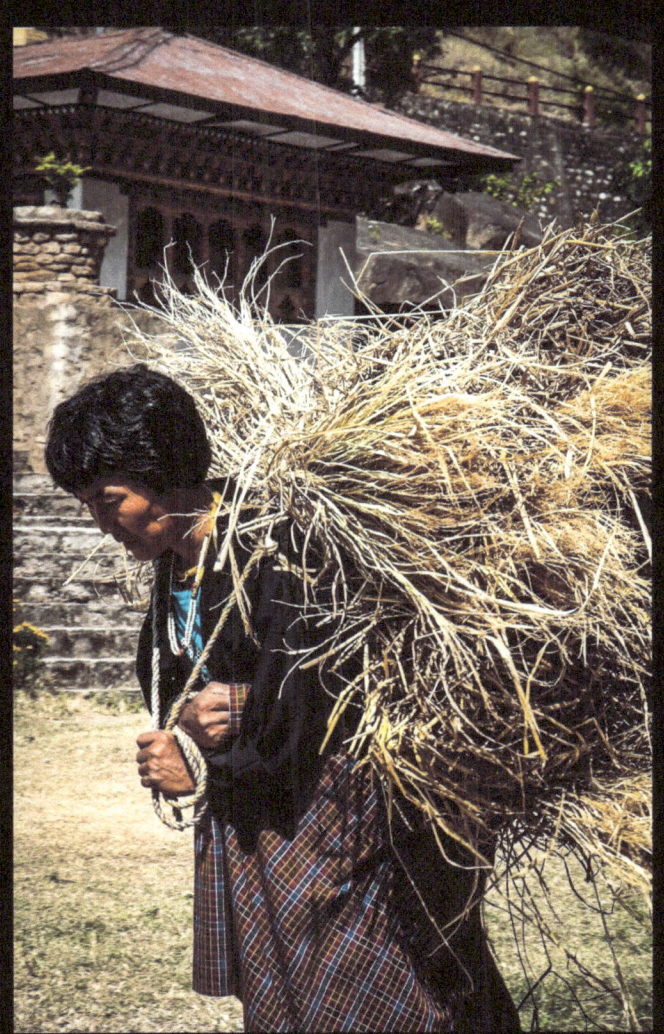

"People travel to faraway places to watch in fascination the kind of people they ignore at home."

-- Dagobert Runes

"There is nothing noble in being
superior to your fellow man;
true nobility is being superior to your
former self."

-- Ernest Hemingway

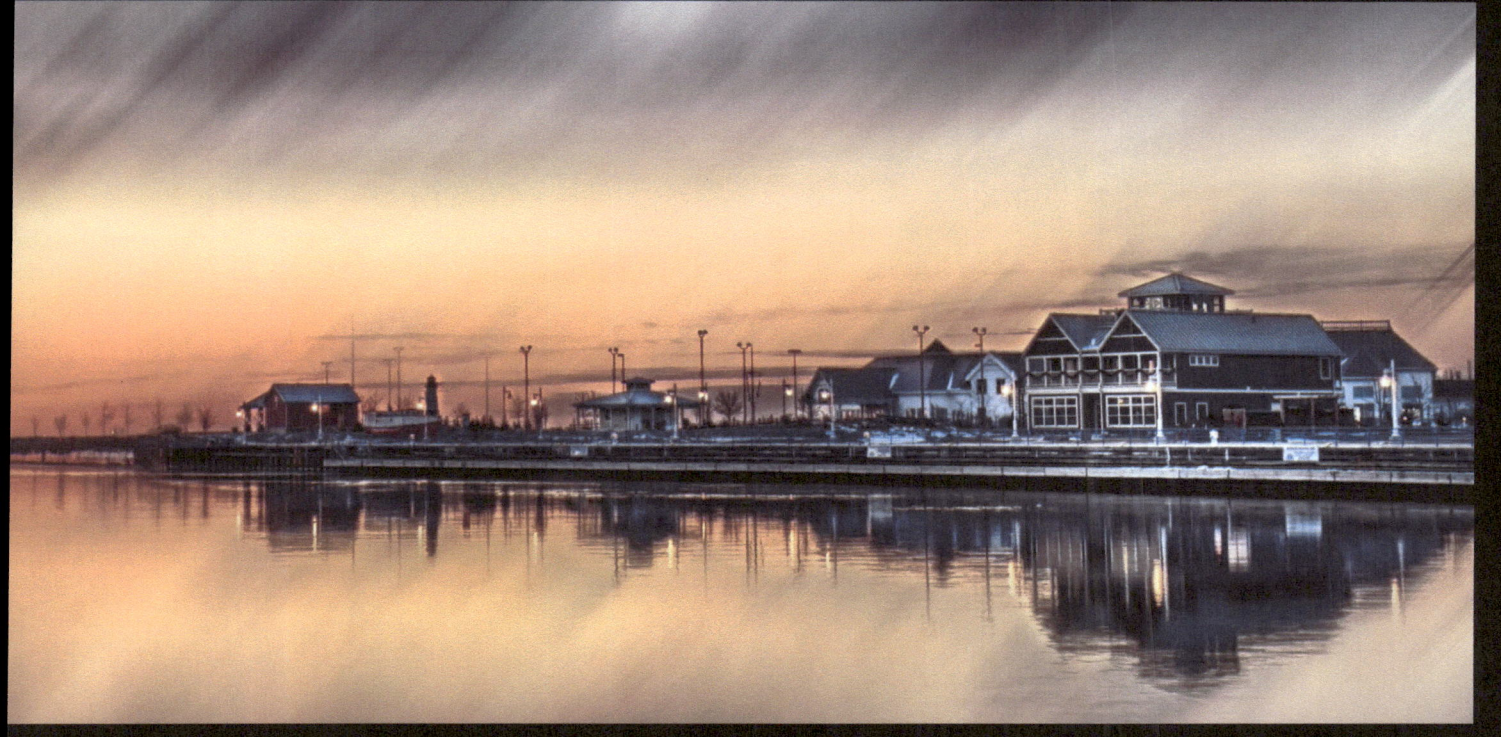

"Don't ask yourself what the world needs,
ask yourself what makes you come alive.
And then go and do that. Because what the
world needs is people who have come alive."

-- Harold Whitman

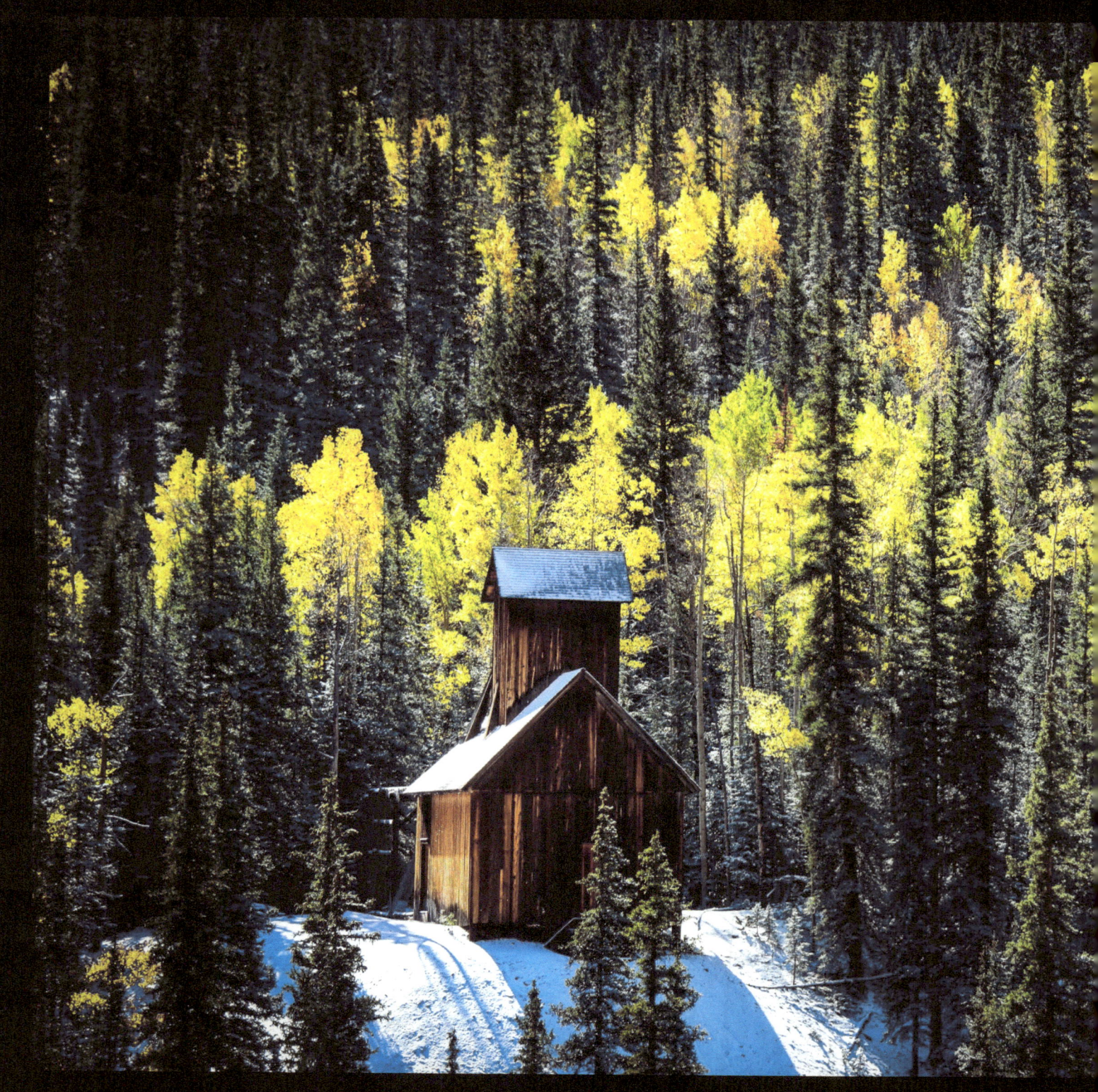

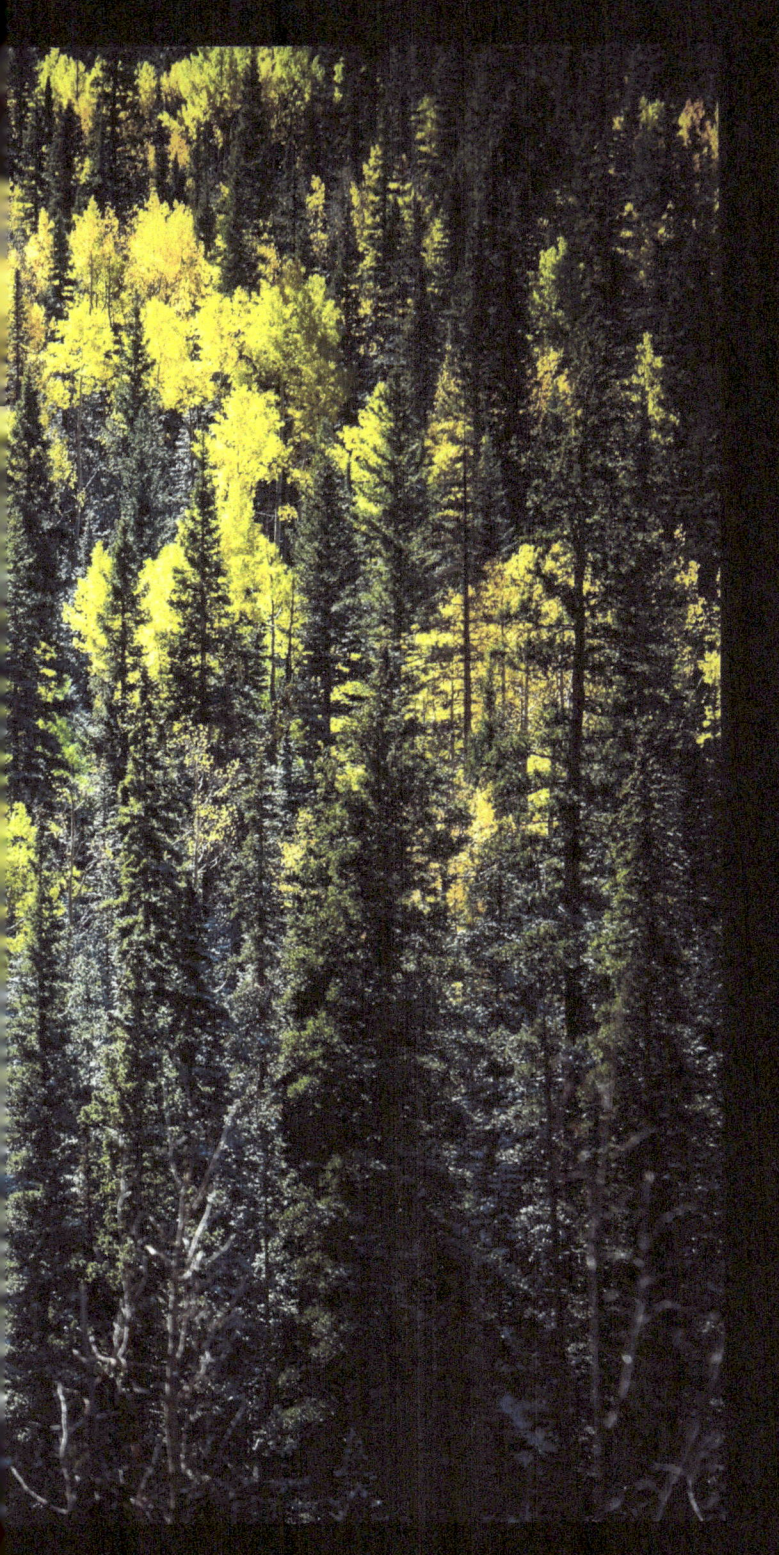

"In every walk
with nature,
one receives
far more than
he seeks."

-- John Muir

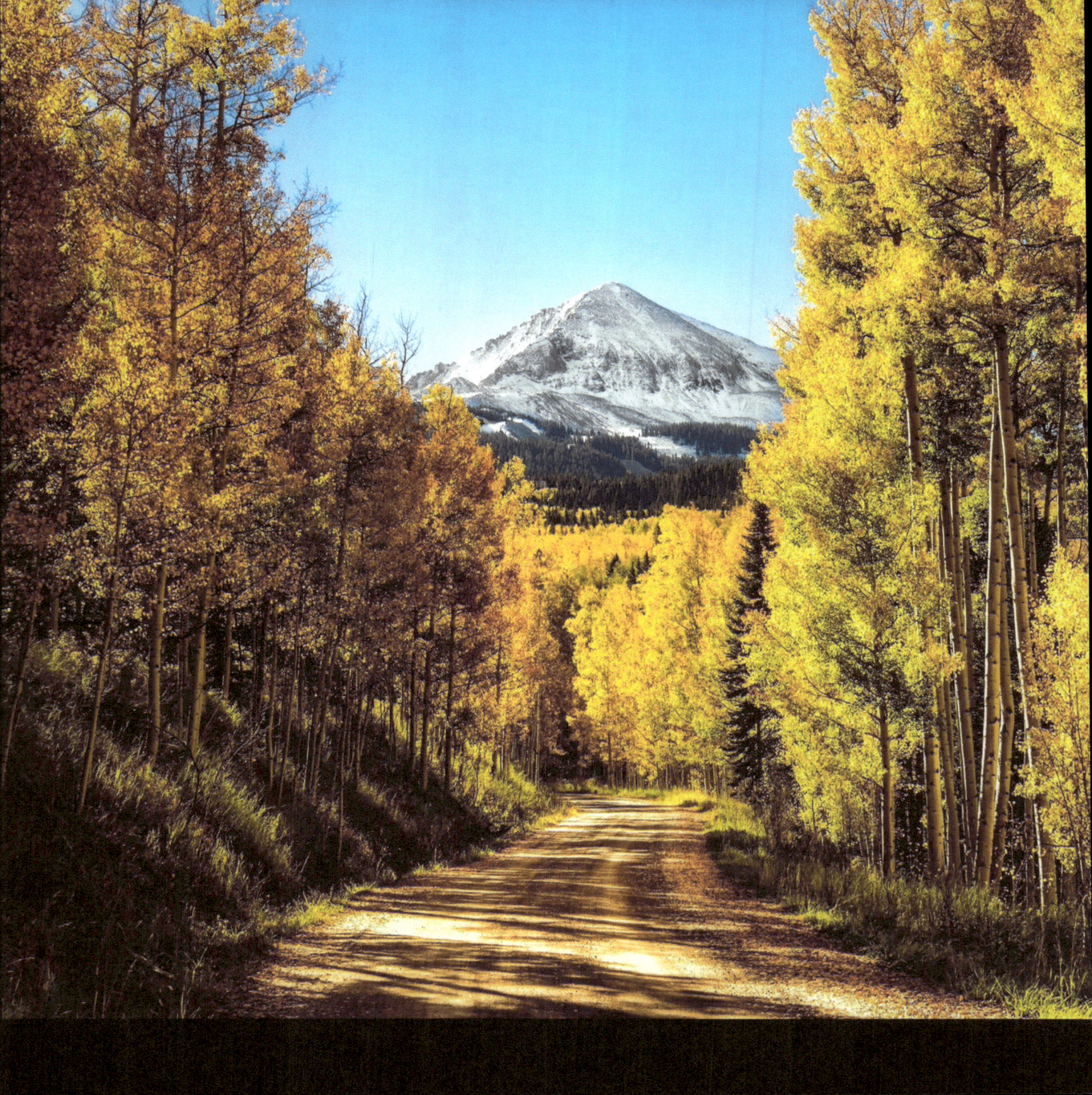

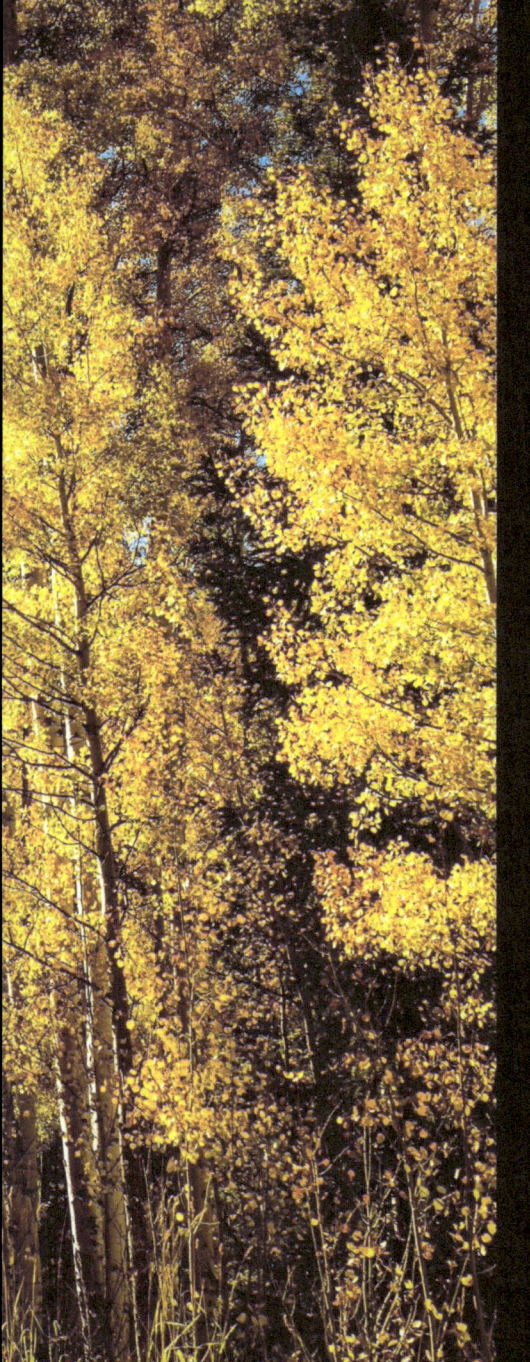

"If one advances confidently in the direction of his dreams, and endeavors to live the life which he imagined, he will meet with success unexpectedly in common hours."

-- Henry David Tho[reau]

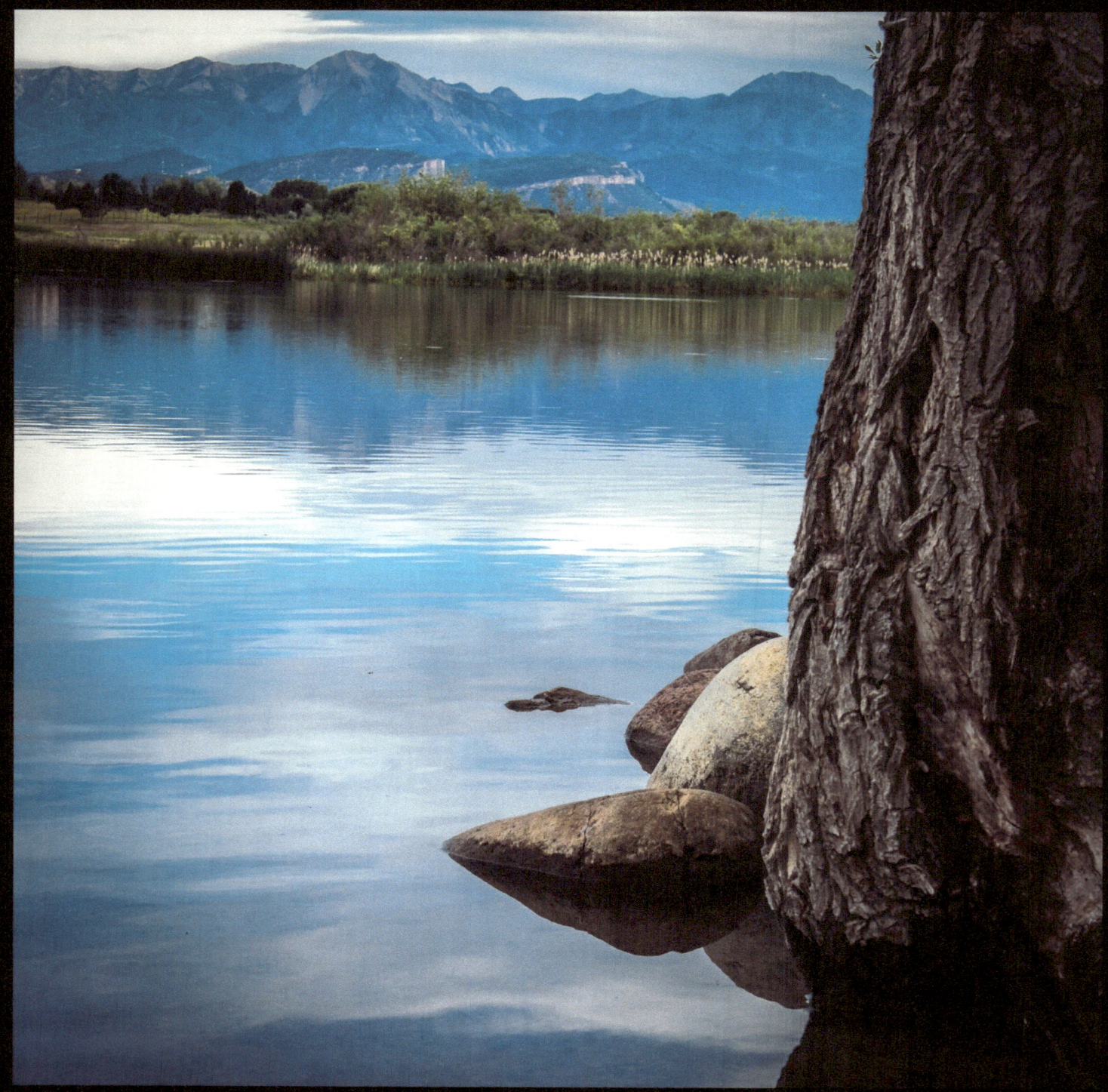

"Whatever you can do
or dream, begin it.
Boldness has genius,
power and magic in it."

-- Goethe

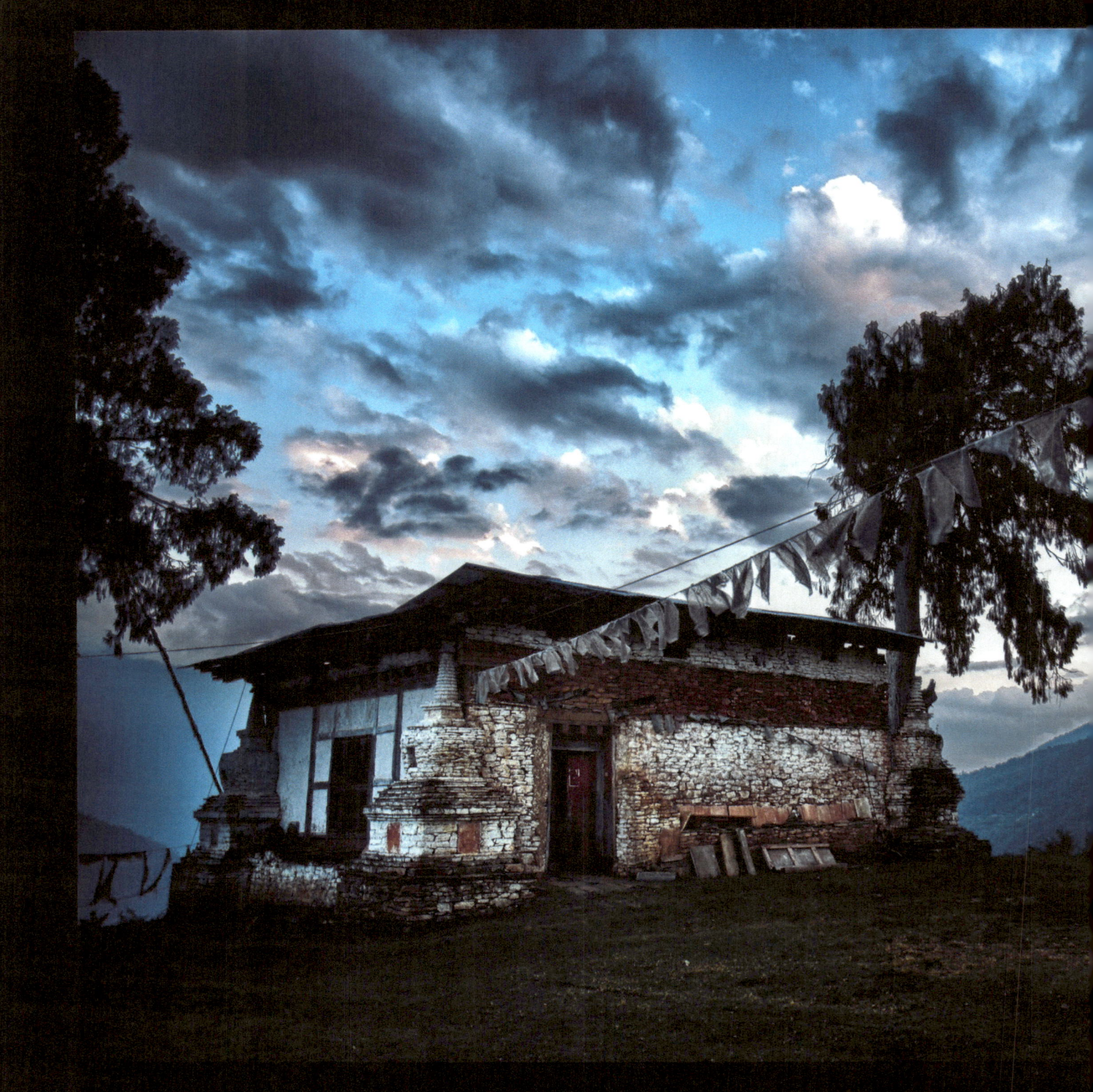

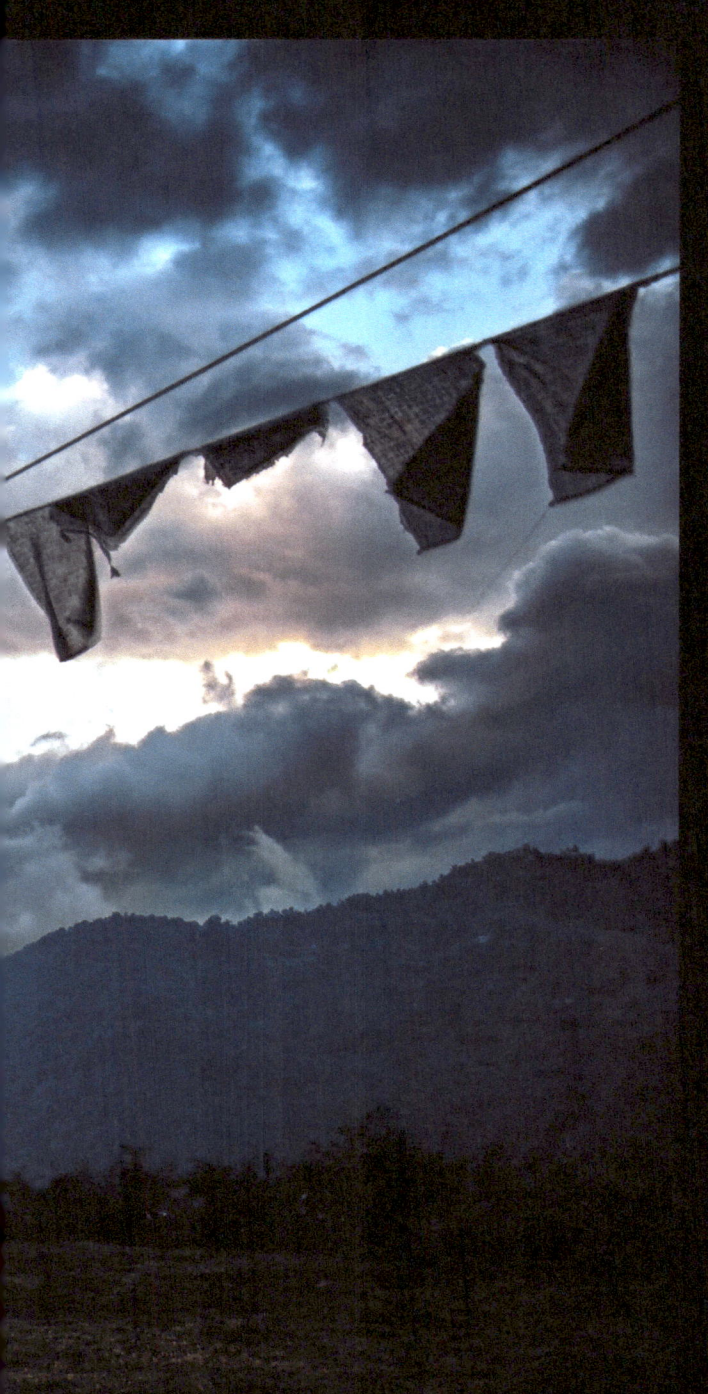

"It is one of the most beautiful compensations of this life that no man can sincerely try to help another without helping himself."

-- Ralph Waldo Emerson

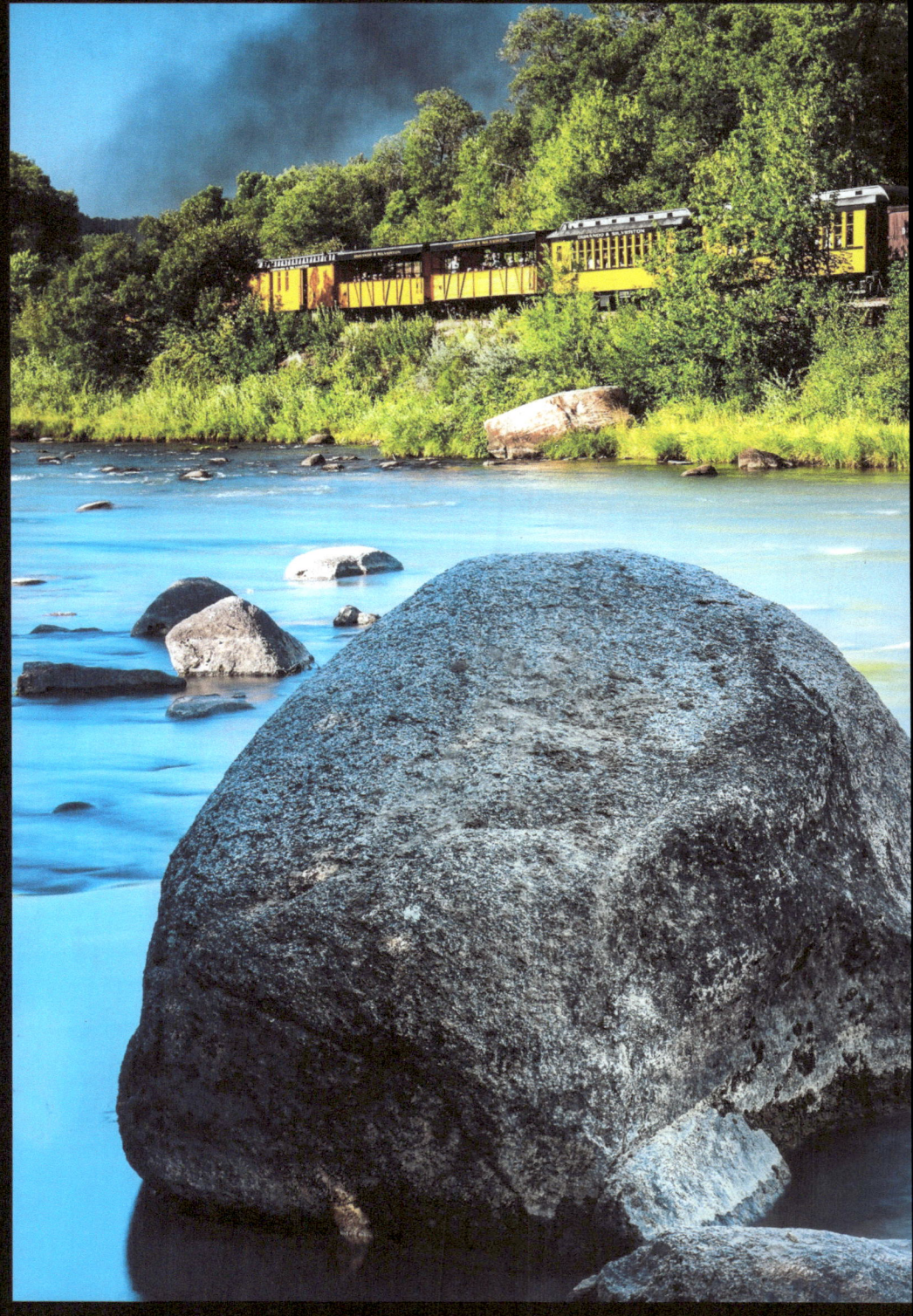

Travel is not reward for work, it's education for living.

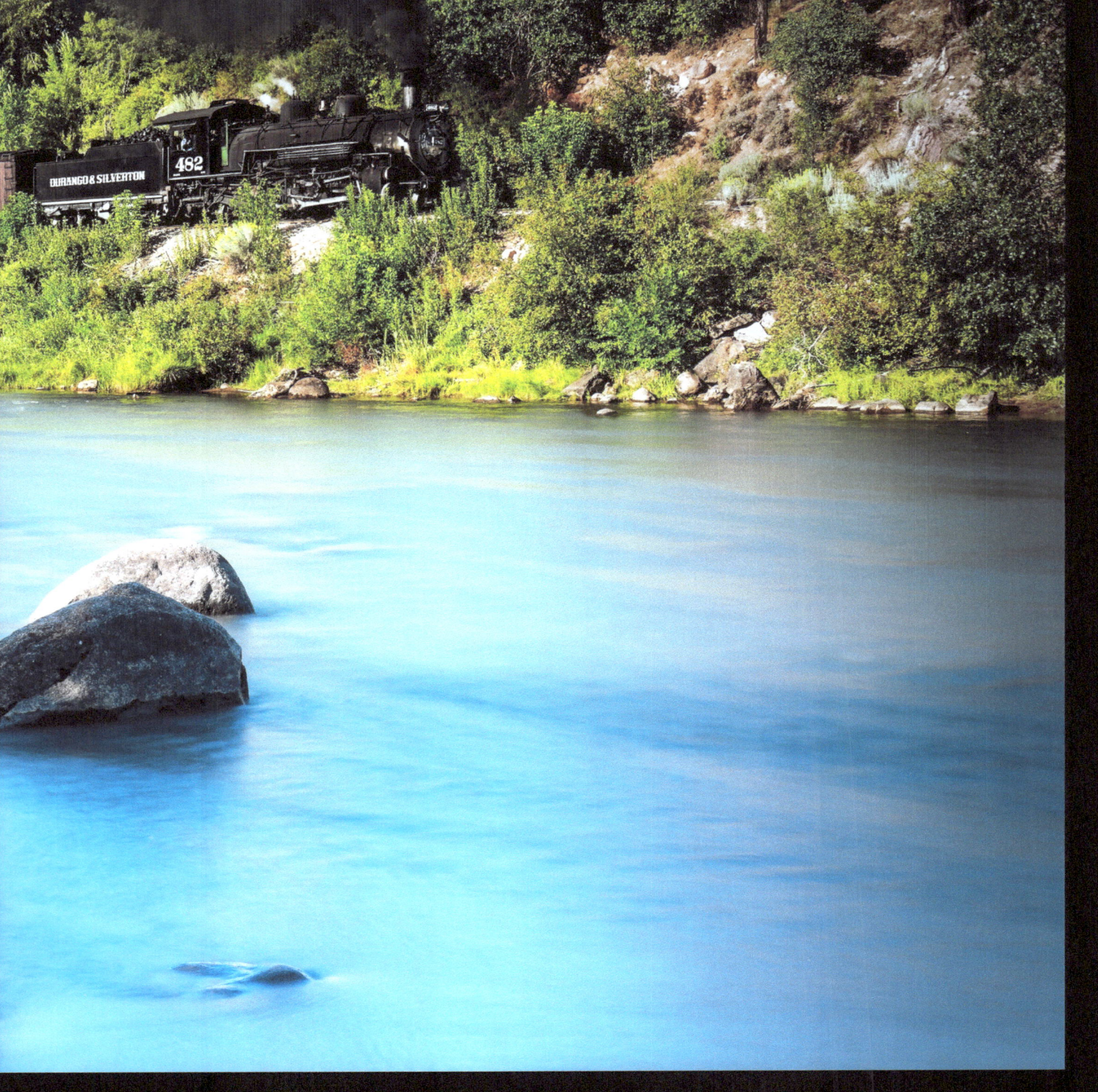

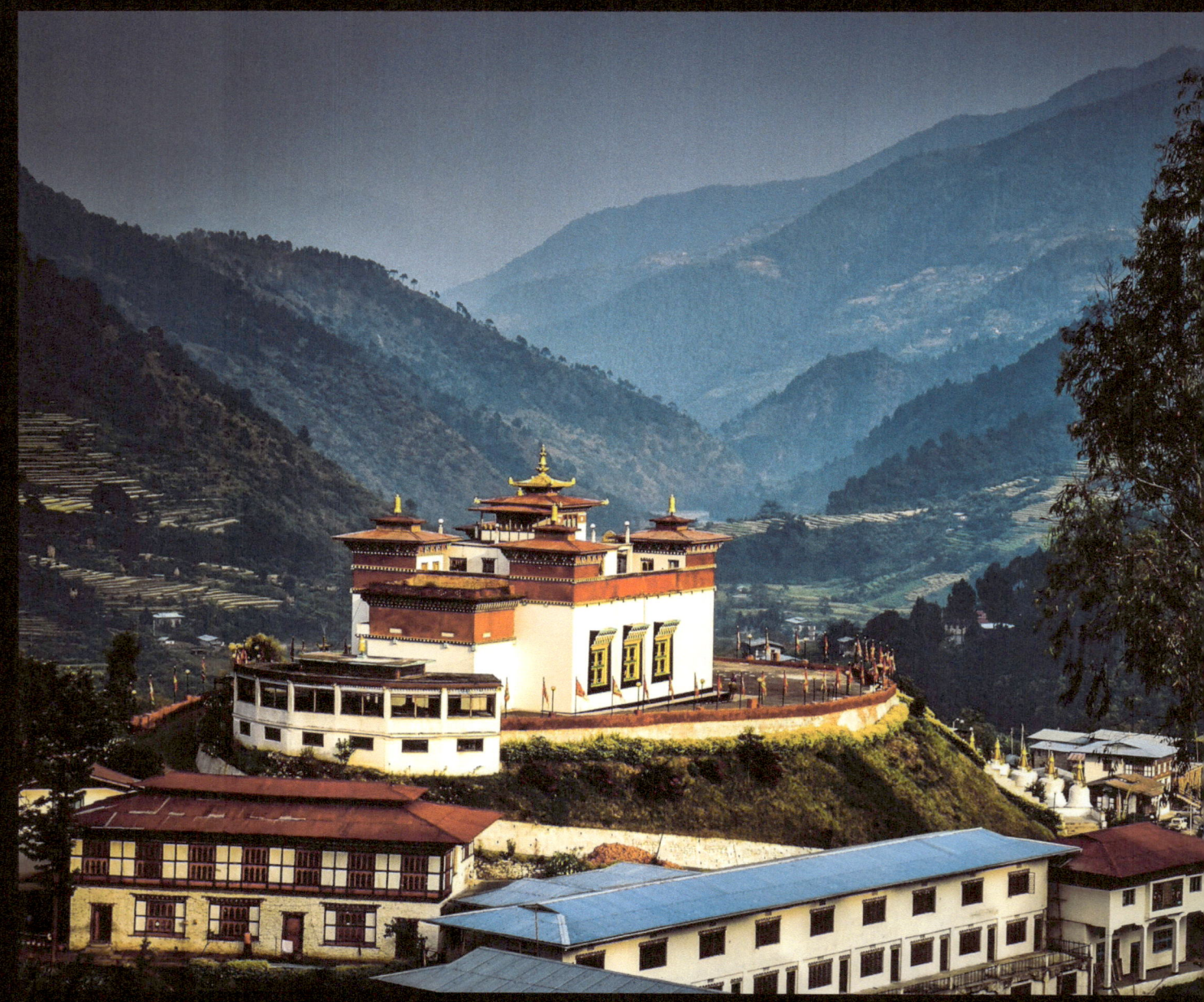

"The real voyage of discovery consists not in seeking new landscapes, but in having new eyes."

--Marcel Proust

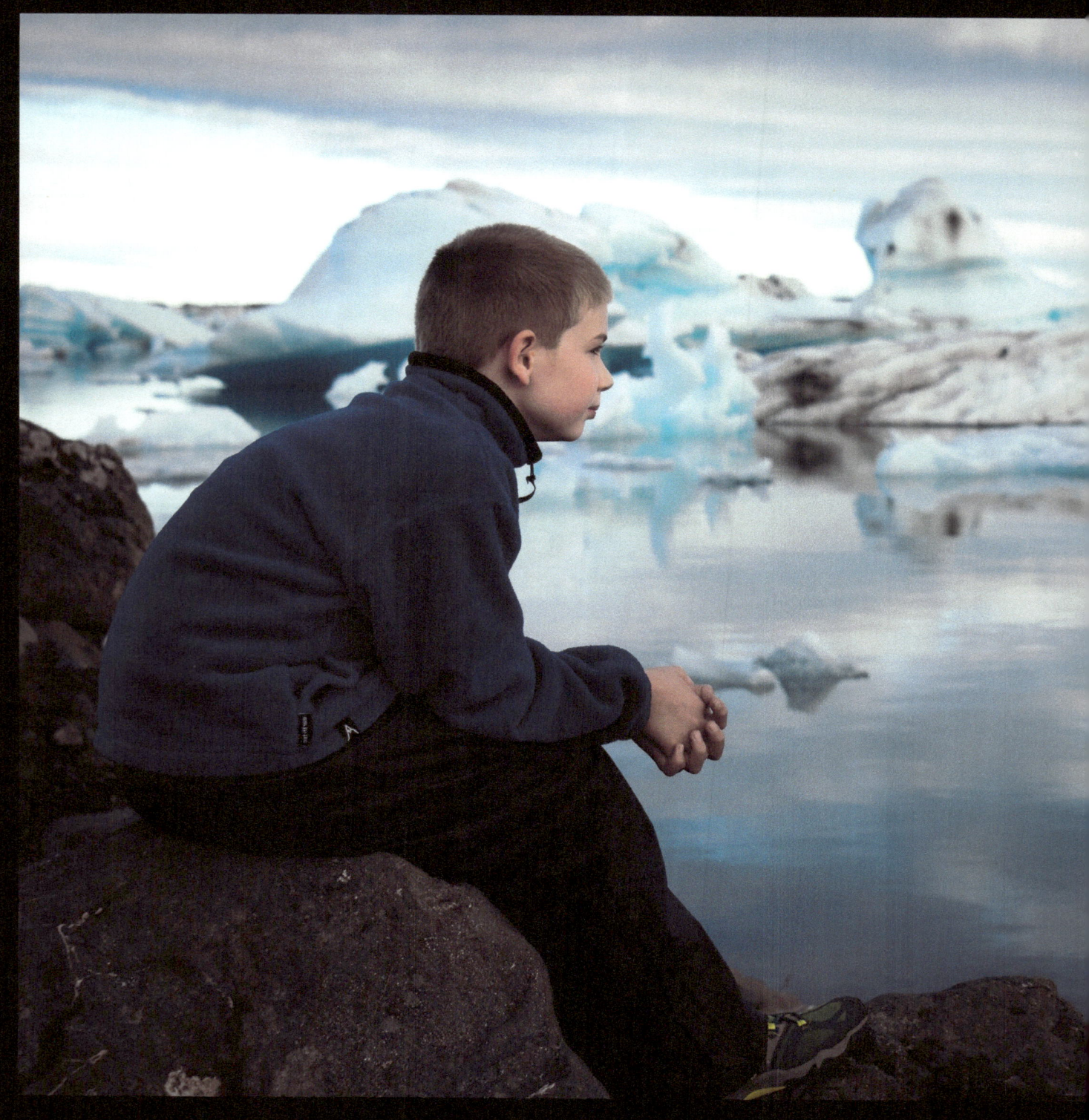

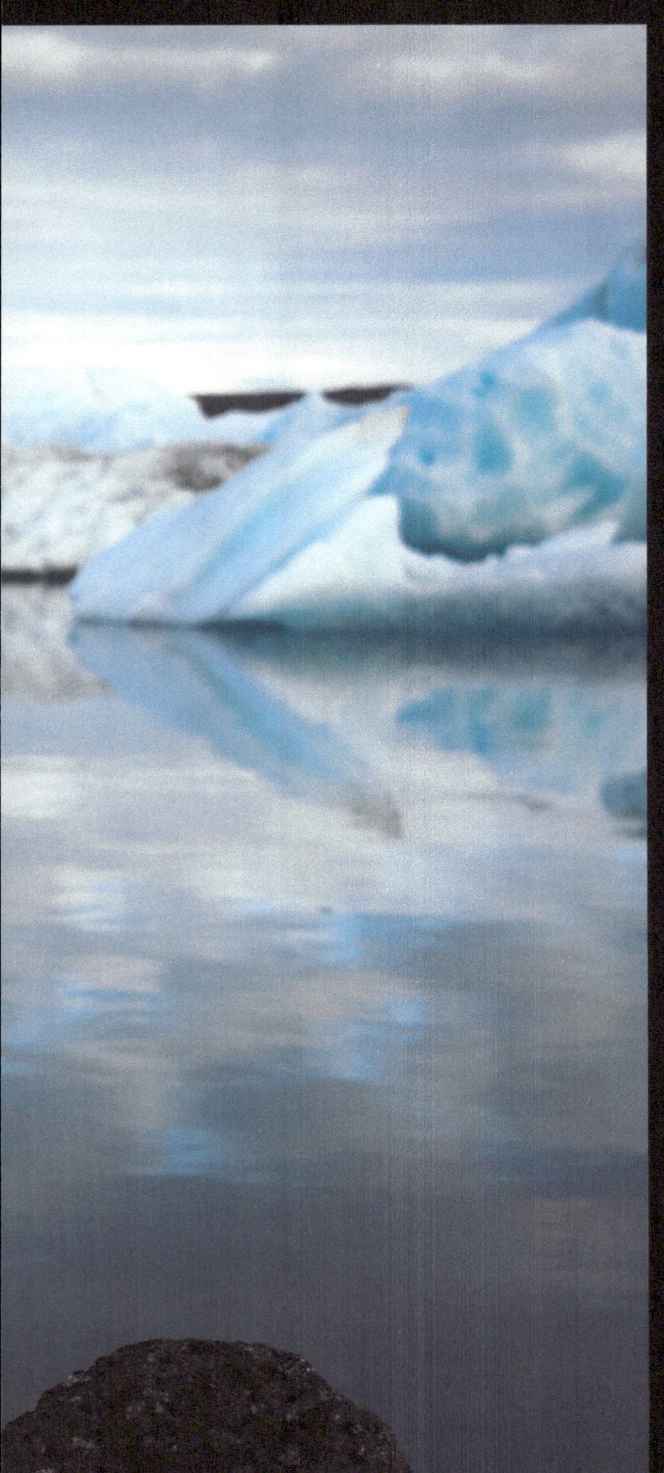

"Not till we are lost. . . .
do we begin to
find ourselves."

-- Henry David Thoreau

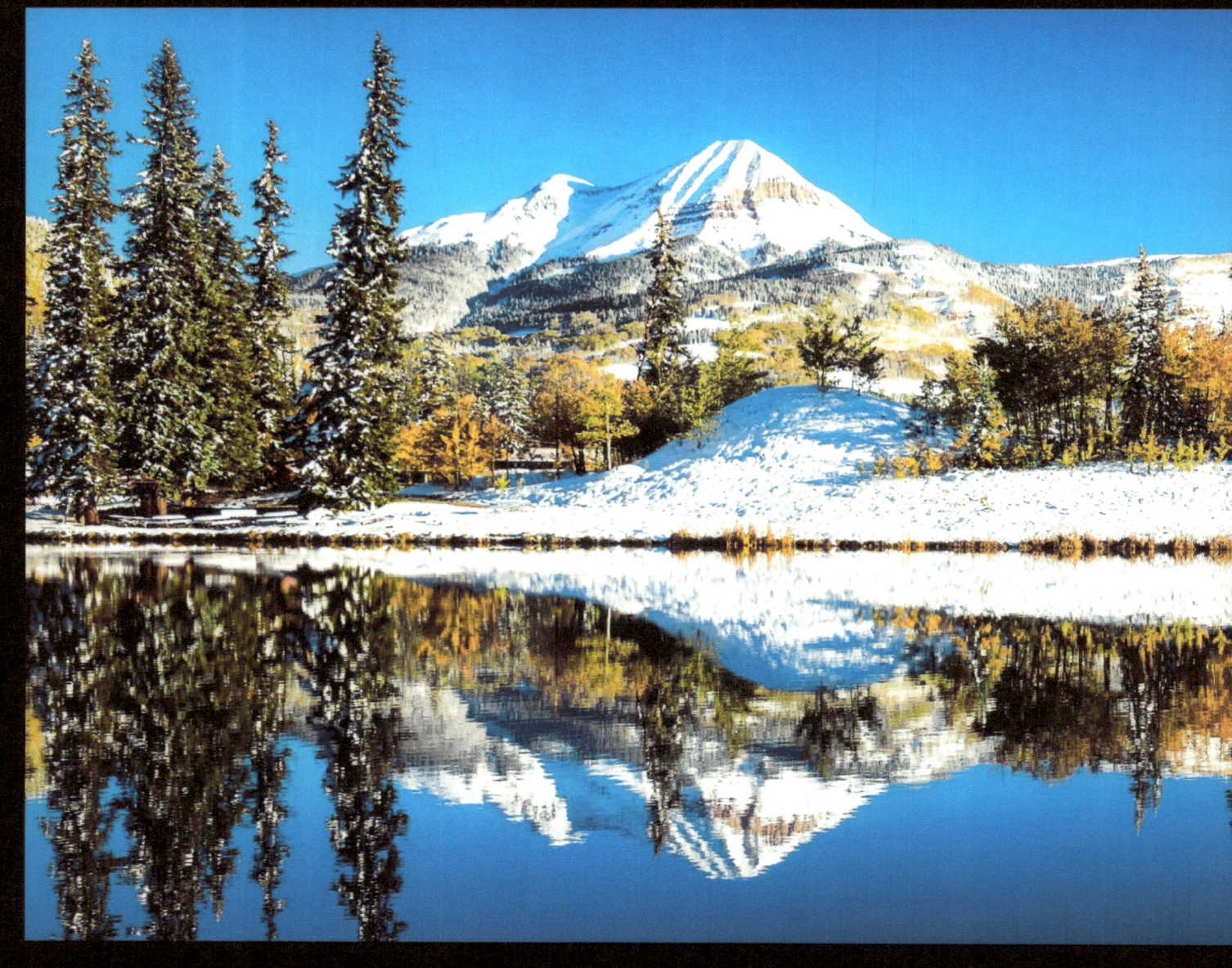

"The influence of fine scenery, the
presence of mountains,

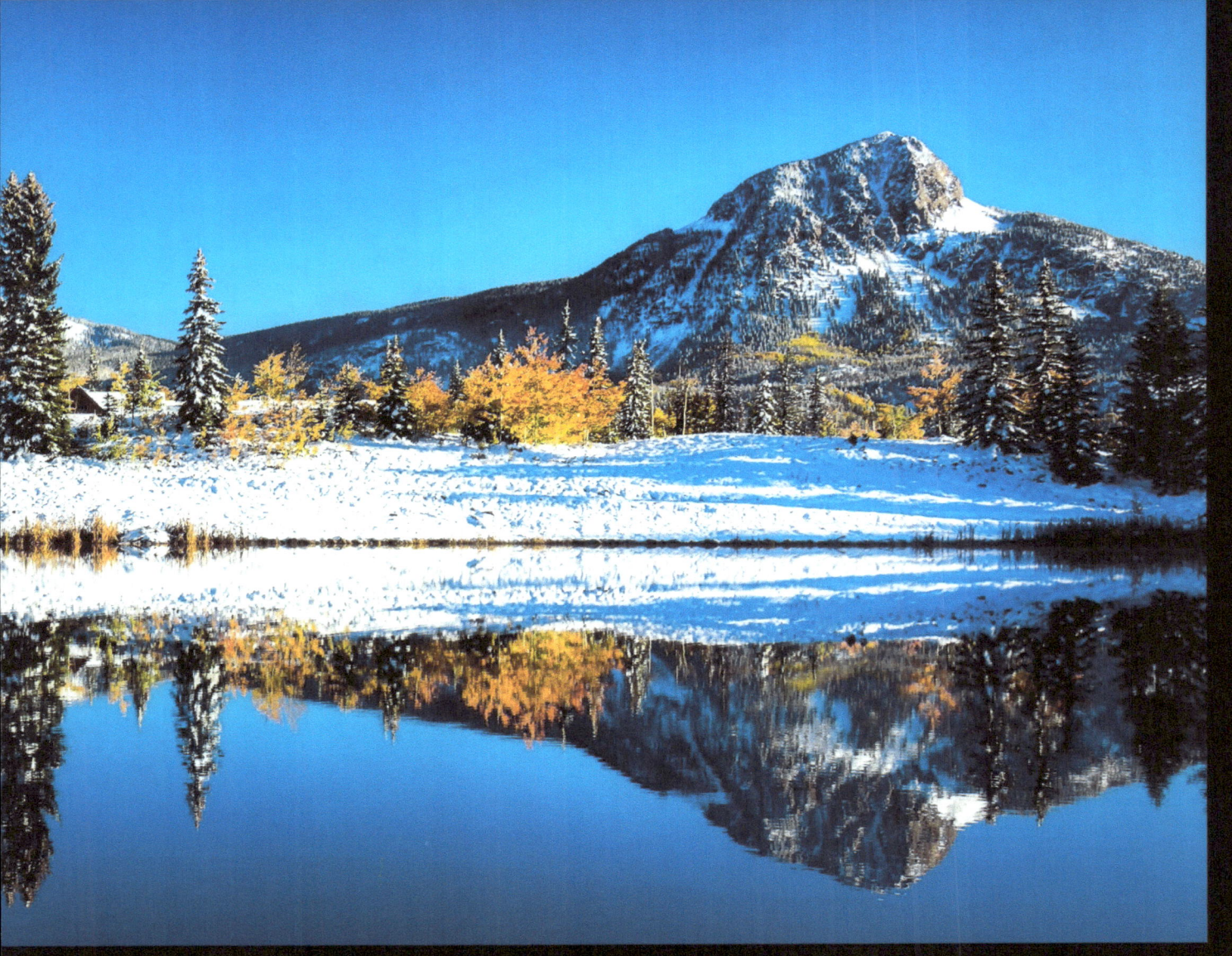

appeases our irritations and
elevates our friendships."
-- Ralph Waldo Emerson

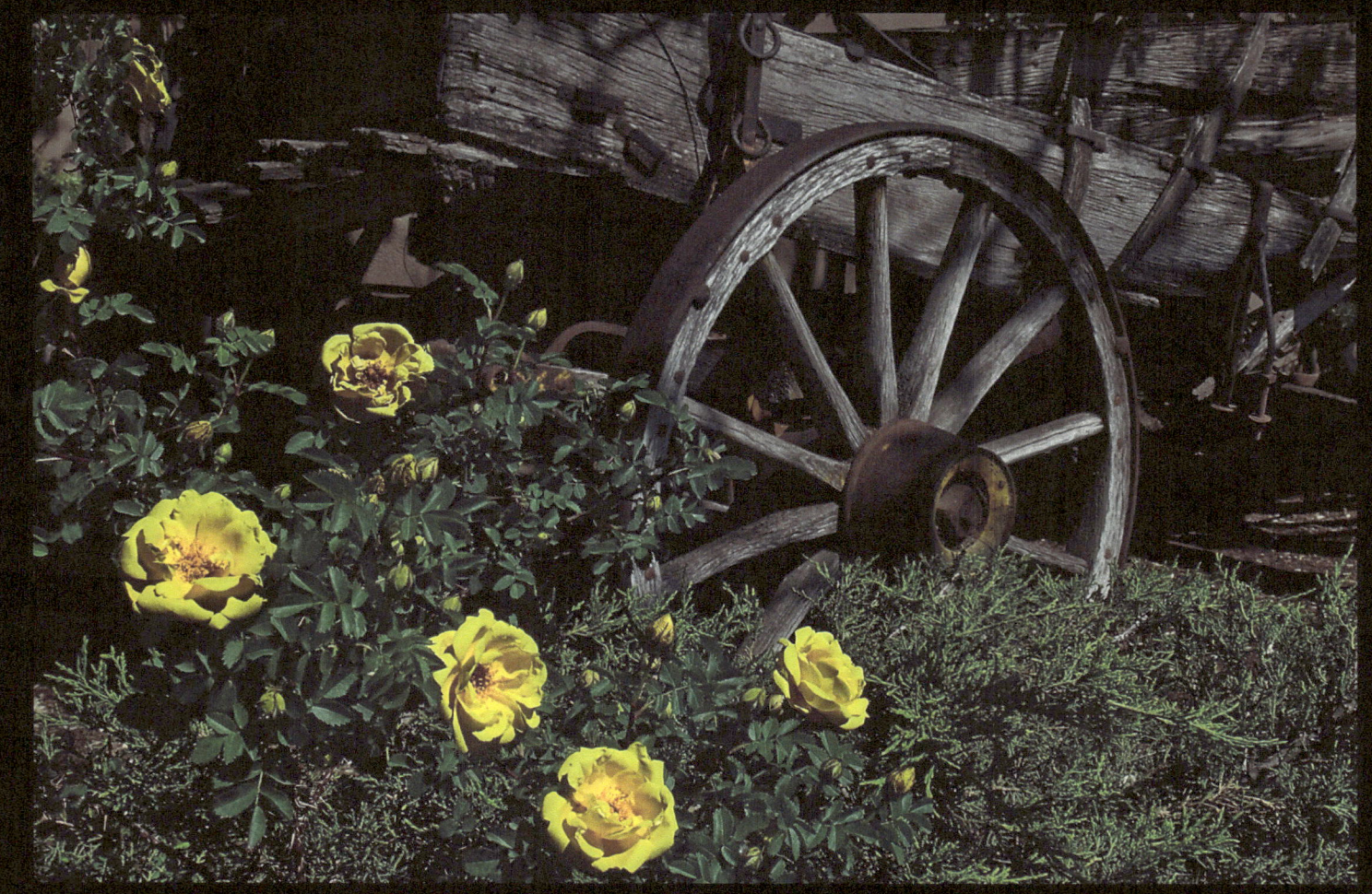

"Everything has its beauty,
but not everyone can see it."

-- Confucius

There are no answers,
only interesting questions.

-- Unknown

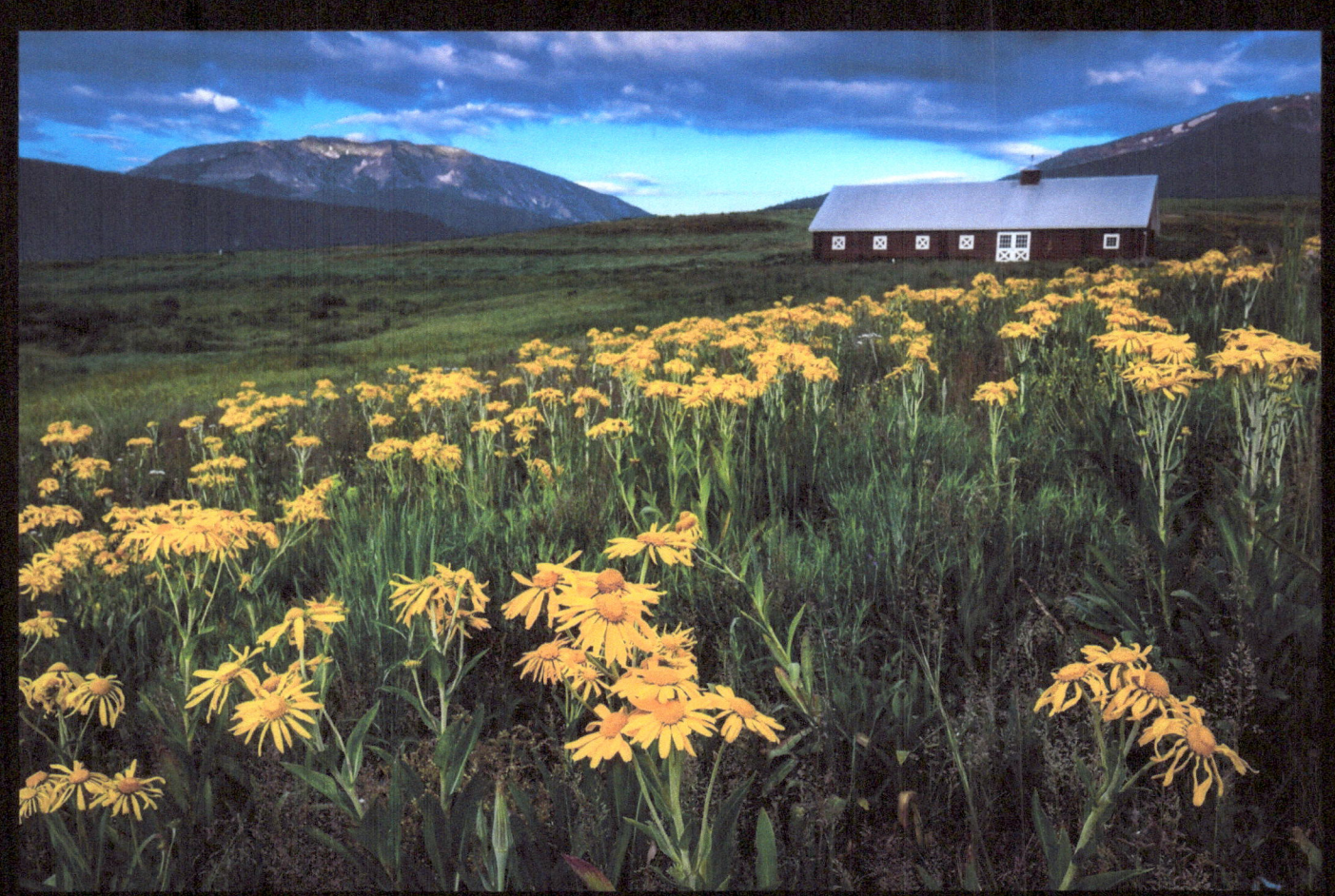

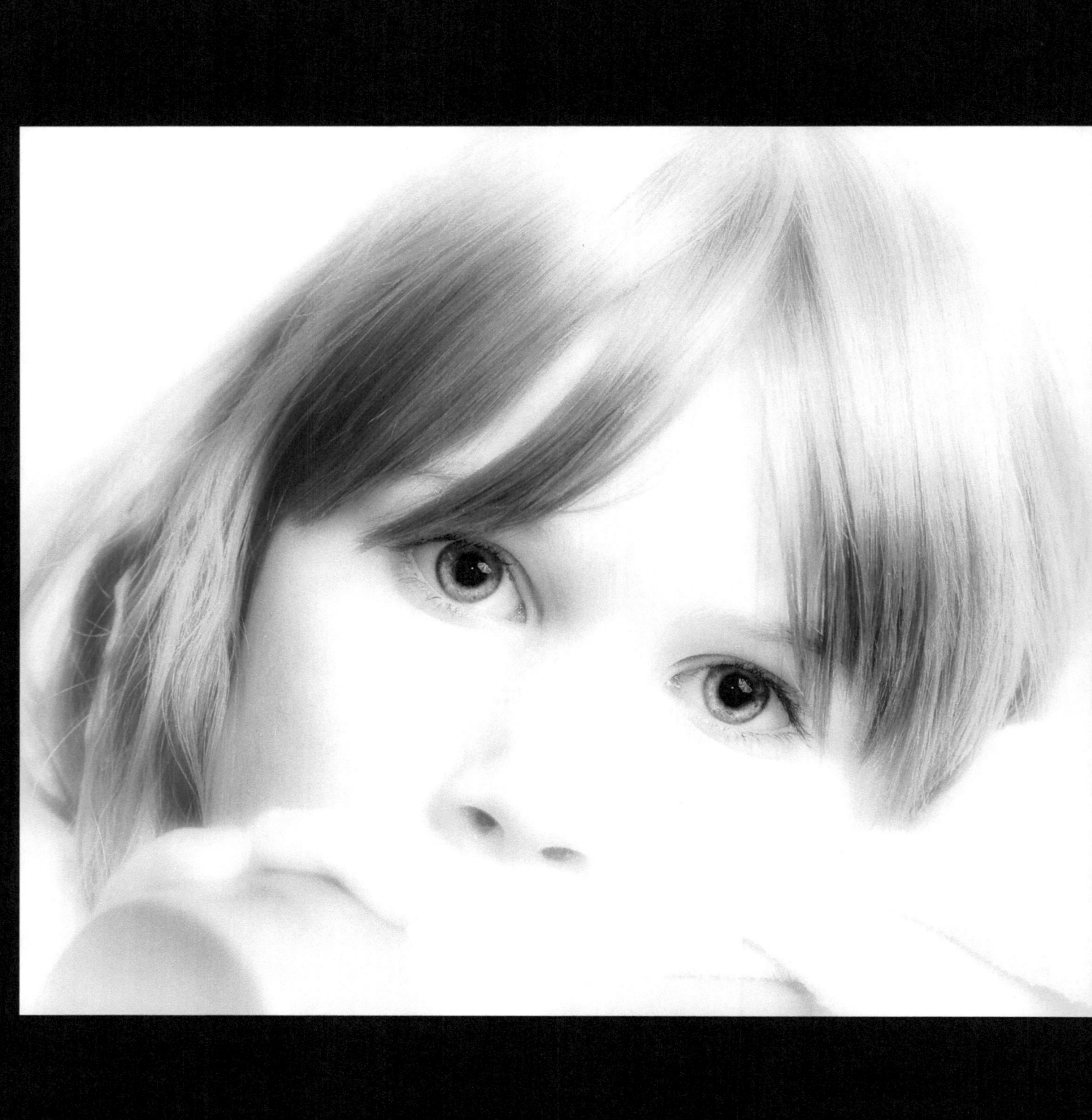

"Simplicity is the
ultimate sophistication."

-- Leonardo da Vinci

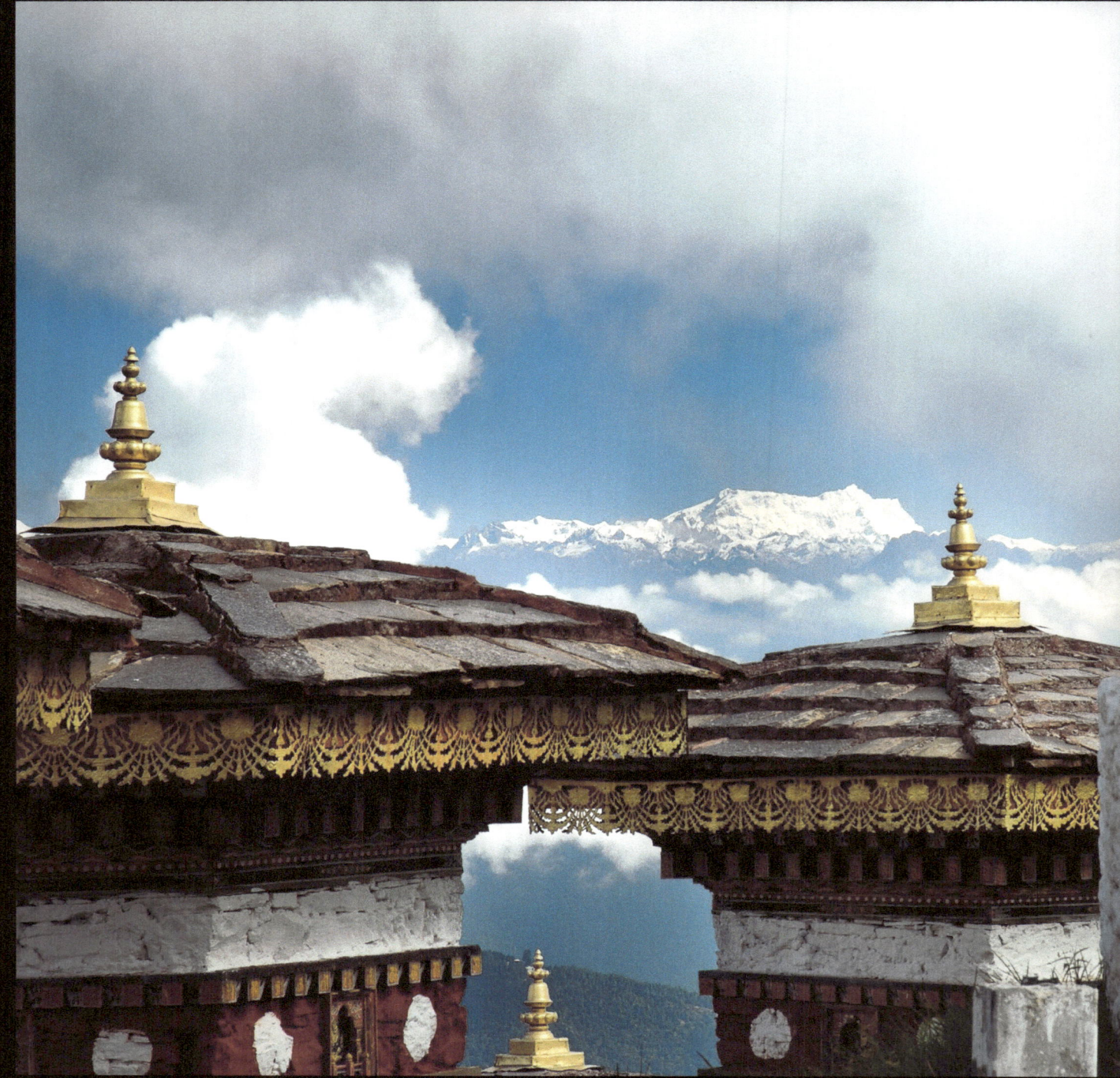

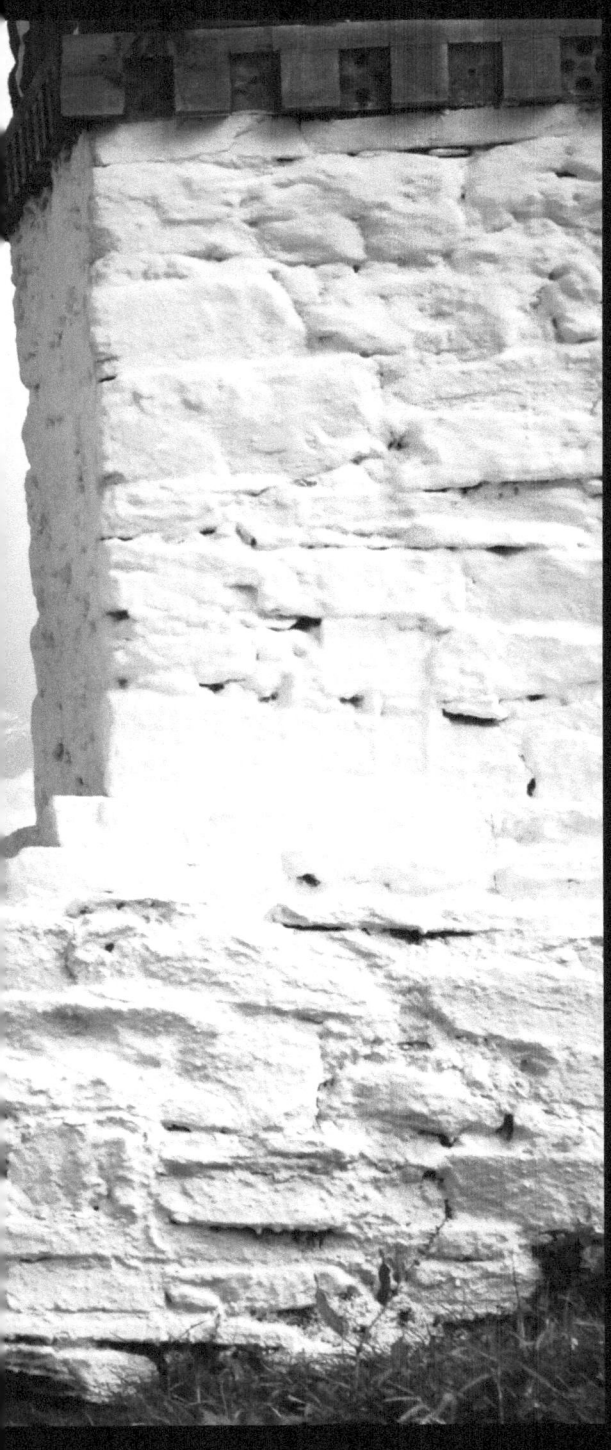

"Invest in your life
experience.
Collect memories,
not material.
Expand your global
perspective."

--Principles of Canadian
Himalayan Expeditions

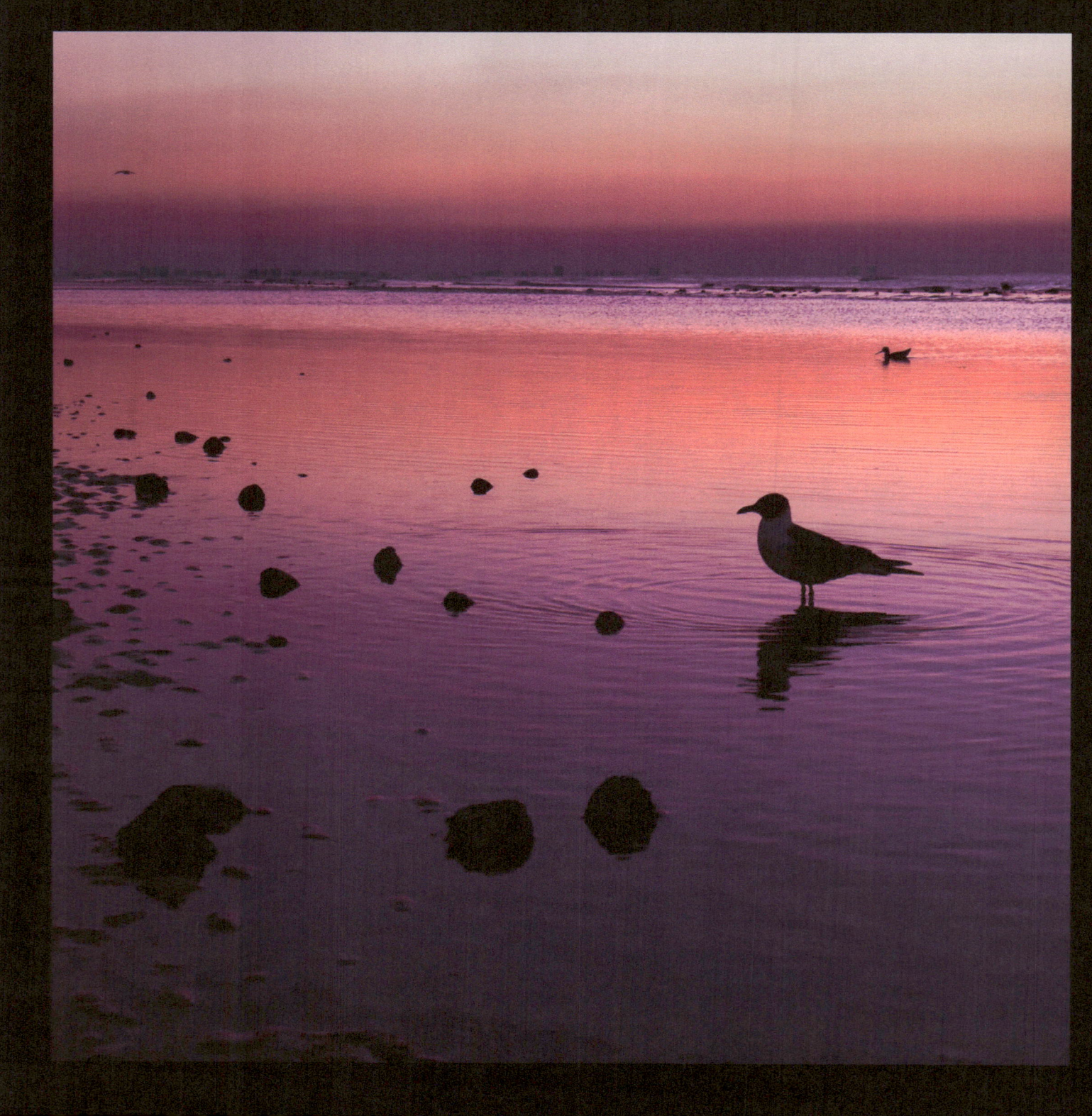

"Brave people don't live forever, but cautious people don't live at all."

--Sir. Richard Branson

"May you live all the
days of your life."

-- Jonathan Swift

www.ingramcontent.com/pod-product-compliance
Lightning Source LLC
Chambersburg PA
CBHW050751180526
45159CB00003B/1418